Intellectual Foreplay

❖

ABOUT THE AUTHORS

Eve Eschner Hogan, MA, is an inspirational speaker and educator. In addition to *Intellectual Foreplay*, she is the author of *The Way of the Winding Path* and co-author of *Rings of Truth*. Eve has a contagious enthusiasm and a charismatic ability to inspire. Through her books and seminars, she has helped thousands of people to discover their inner resources, thus expanding their awareness and strengthening their life skills. Eve's specialty is in relationship enhancement whether the relationship is with yourself, your sweetheart, your family or with God. She lives on the island of Maui with her husband, Steven, where she also serves as a counselor, labyrinth facilitator and wedding officiant.

Steven Hogan, boat captain, scuba instructor and underwater cinematographer, is the owner of Makena Coast Charters on Maui. He is the co-producer of the video, *Whales, Turtles and Dolphins: Ambassadors of the Sea*. Eve and Steven's co-creation of the concept and practice of *Intellectual Foreplay* led to their mutually supportive marriage.

Dedicated to Samantha,

a loving and wise young woman;

may you lead the way in this generation

of people who use their heads and their hearts

for creating healthy, loving relationships.

ORDERING

Trade bookstores in the U.S. and Canada please contact:

Publishers Group West
1700 Fourth Street, Berkeley CA 94710
Phone: (800) 788-3123   Fax: (510) 528-3444

Hunter House books are available at bulk discounts for textbook course adoptions; to qualifying community, healthcare, and government organizations; and for special promotions and fundraising. For details please contact:

Special Sales Department
Hunter House Inc., PO Box 2914, Alameda CA 94501-0914
Phone: (510) 865-5282   Fax: (510) 865-4295
e-mail: ordering@hunterhouse.com

Individuals can order our books from most bookstores or by calling toll-free: **1-800-266-5592**

Intellectual Foreplay

QUESTIONS FOR LOVERS
AND LOVERS-TO-BE

❖

Eve Eschner Hogan, M.A.,
with Steven Hogan

Hunter House
PUBLISHERS

Hunter House Inc., Publishers
P.O. Box 2914
Alameda CA 94501-0914

LIBRARY OF CONGRESS CATALOGING-IN-PUBLICATION DATA

Hogan, Eve Eschner, 1961-
 Intellectual foreplay: questions for lovers and lovers to be / Eve Eschner
 Hogan with Steven Hogan.—1st ed.
  p. cm.
 ISBN 0-89793-277-3 (paper)
  1. Mate selection. 2. Interpersonal communication. I. Hogan, Steven. II.
  Title.
HQ801 .H66 2000
646.7'7—dc21   99-059325

PROJECT CREDITS

COVER DESIGN: Madeleine Budnick Designs
BOOK DESIGN AND PRODUCTION: Brian Dittmar Graphic Design
DEVELOPMENT AND COPYEDITING: Laura Harger
PROOFREADER: Susan Burckhard
PRODUCTION DIRECTOR: Virginia Fontana
ACQUISITIONS COORDINATOR: Jeanne Brondino
EDITORIAL INTERN: Dory Cleveland
PUBLICITY DIRECTOR: Marisa Spatafore
SPECIAL SALES MANAGER: Sarah Kulin
CUSTOMER SERVICE MANAGER: Christina Sverdrup
ORDER FULFILLMENT: A & A Quality Shipping Services, Joel Irons
PUBLISHER: Kiran S. Rana

9 8 7 6 5 4   First Edition   03 04

Printed in Canada

Contents

❖

❖

Acknowledgements

e wish to thank the multitude of people who contributed to this book in numerous ways, especially by sharing questions, concerns, stories, and topics.

Thanks to the Eschner family for the unending encouragement and support. The most special of thanks to Lauralyn Eschner for her brilliance in thinking of the title, *Intellectual Foreplay* ... to Meg and Al Eschner for modeling the meaning of unconditional love ... and to Ed, Wendy, and Amy Eschner for your love and faith. Thanks also to the Hogan family for your warm acceptance and encouragement. You are all so wonderful, and we love you so much!

Jack Canfield, for your mentorship and friendship over the last several years. You, my friend, have truly made a difference! Thank you!

Jane Foley, for pushing me out into the world and being such an awesome, generous, loving best friend. Your presence and energy have kept me going when I might not have continued. Thanks to Mike Foley, too, for sharing Jane so sweetly; your love and support are appreciated more than you can imagine.

Bob Adjemian, for your unending support, encouragement, contacts, and ideas, which have truly been instrumental in making this happen.

Wendee Mason, founder of Date Smart Seminars, for your continued enthusiasm and use of *Intellectual Foreplay* in your classes. Thank you for sharing the stories and ideas. You are an inspiration.

All the people, many of whom we met through Income Builders International, who have offered contacts, ideas, and encouragement, most especially Berny, Lynn and Tony Dohrmann, David Rose, Brenda Rose, Enrico Melson, Cloudsifter Flood, Barry Spilchuk, Vincent Molina, Rob Wickstrom, Bruce Moffatt, Dana Hirsch and the many others who purchased the book and shared in the enthusiasm—too many to name on these pages, but all of whom are acknowledged in our hearts.

The team at Hunter House for having faith and being so wonderful to work with! A special thanks to Laura Harger—a masterful editor!

Most, most, most ... Steven, thank you for the hours and hours you spent exploring and researching the questions and engaging in *Intellectual Foreplay* with me as we discovered our path together. Your support means the world to me. I love you.

To my beloved Gurus, who guide me each step of the way. Baba, S. S., and the rest—thank you for the unending love and blessings.

Introduction

*"Judge people by their questions
rather than their answers."*
—VOLTAIRE

n the early stages of our courtship, my husband, Steven, and I were involved in a long-distance relationship. We met when I was on vacation on Maui, where he lived. We spent a week enjoying each other's company and then I returned to California. Although we were three thousand miles apart, our courtship continued, over the telephone. ("It's the next best thing to being there . . . .") It soon became evident that in order for us to be together, one of us would have to move. Neither of us wanted to make that kind of commitment unless we were pretty sure we were making the right choice, so we started asking each other questions. After coming up with questions several nights in a row, Steven let me know that it was now my turn to ask him questions. Somewhat jokingly, we agreed my "turn to ask" would be the next evening's phone call.

Thus it began. Suddenly, I realized I wasn't sure what I truly needed to know. While considering the upcoming phone call, I casually asked everyone I knew, "What should you ask someone before you get seriously involved?" To my surprise, everyone had an answer! Before long I had a lengthy list of questions—written on napkins, the back of receipts, anything available. The questions ranged from bathroom habits to deep spiritual philosophies to practical lifestyle inquiries. Finding the variety of questions fascinating, I kept asking, and the list kept growing. Unknowingly, we had begun the compilation of this book. Putting the list of questions to the test, we took it to the telephone and explored the myriad topics together, adding to it nightly.

In essence, we engaged in *Intellectual Foreplay* in our relationship, which led to me moving to Maui and marrying Steven. It was then that it occurred to us that other people might need assistance in that "getting-to-know-each-other" stage, too. Since Steven owns a scuba-diving company on Maui, he continued to gather questions by interviewing his customers each day on the boat, while I added some valuable concepts for raising self-esteem and developing healthy relationships to the text.

Soon, our friends started asking for copies of the "book" to use with their dates. Even though it wasn't in finished form, the demand was so high that I started copying the rough draft and selling it to those who asked. Word spread quickly. Soon people we didn't even know were asking for copies of *Intellectual Foreplay,* so I self-published a working version of the book, selling it at workshops and via word of mouth. Other workshop facilitators started ordering it for their classes, and it soon became obvious that I needed to find a publisher to keep up with the demand!

I have since revised the book to include additional information and questions, as well as the many stories that people have shared with us over the years that *Intellectual Foreplay* has been in development. The compilation of these ideas, questions and stories has resulted in the book that follows. And for us, the development of *Intellectual Foreplay* resulted in our choosing the right partner.

What Is Intellectual Foreplay?

"Foreplay" literally means "the play that comes first," the play that you engage in before you go the distance together. We generally think of this in physical terms: foreplay builds intrigue, excitement, and desire—creating readiness—before sex. Foreplay is time well spent, because it makes the whole experience more satisfying. *Intellectual Foreplay* offers a variation on this idea: it is the stimulation and interest that is sparked between two people when they communicate intimately. Just like its physical counterpart,

Intellectual Foreplay can build excitement and desire—or quickly reveal a lack of compatibility, saving you months, or even years, of developing a relationship that isn't going to work.

Intellectual Foreplay asks you to use your head and your heart before sharing your body and your life. We are all aware of the immediate power of physical attraction and its ability to vanish once we get to know someone better or to linger long after any traces of a healthy relationship remain. The compatibility that is developed through truly knowing someone before getting seriously involved can increase attraction and facilitate the longevity and quality of the union. This well-spent time can simply make your relationship better, stronger, and more satisfying.

By learning all you can about your partner, discussing issues before they become problems, revealing unexpressed agreements and assumptions, and looking deeply at what matters to you, your chances of making the right choice of partner will greatly increase. You cannot be a victim of ignorance when you go into a relationship conscious, knowing your choices. *Intellectual Foreplay* will also help you to make choices *within* the relationship that will keep love alive, helping you to avoid the painful experience of breaking up.

One of the biggest mistakes we make at the beginning of a relationship is *not* asking enough questions. When taking on any other endeavor—a business relationship, buying a house, buying appliances—we wisely ask a whole host of questions to ensure that we make the right choice. Can you imagine buying a house because it looks good and feels good without examining the costs, the condition of the property, serious damage, needed repairs, your readiness to move, your commitment to the payments, the previous owner's readiness to sell, what the neighbors are like, and on and on? Yet that is exactly what we do in relationships. We base our choices solely on physical attraction and emotional desire, and then can't understand why our relationships don't work. *Intellectual Foreplay* is a tool for getting to know yourself and your partner in a deep and practical way, thus enabling you to make healthy, educated decisions.

Times have changed in the realm of relationships, and these changes require a new, more conscious approach toward choosing a partner. When I was a school counselor, some sixth-grade students, two eleven-year-old "couples," came to me upset because the two girls had just broken up with the two boys. When I asked what had happened, the boys explained that they had been "served papers" by the girls, and they went on to tell me why they had broken up. I stopped their explanation to ask what being "served papers" meant. They all got really embarrassed, and then one boy explained that they had been pretending that they were married, so when the girls served them the papers, the age-old game of make-believe marriage was given a new twist: they were now divorced. At age eleven! This is a pretty sad sign of our times. We believe *Intellectual Foreplay* is designed to help you avoid the all-too-common reality of break-up or divorce.

FOURplay

The central idea of *Intellectual Foreplay* is the practice of FOURplay—getting to know each other 1) intellectually, 2) emotionally, 3) spiritually, and 4) physically before making the commitment to serious involvement. Granted, if you think too much about your relationship, you may never get married. However, if you think too little, you'll surely get divorced.

We are all pretty familiar with the standard questions that are usually asked when two people meet: "What's your name?" which is usually followed quickly by, "What do you do?" or "Do you live around here?" And, if we are wise, we try to find out early on whether someone is married or has a partner or a house full of kids. Usually we inquire about these things indirectly, with a question such as, "Do you live alone?" While these are excellent places to start, this is the point where most people stop asking and just start dating. As you'll discover in this book, there is a lot more you can discover about someone (and yourself) by asking more questions!

There are several different lines of questions that can be explored with a new partner. Some are basic getting-to-know-each-other questions, such as:

What is your favorite way to spend your time?

What kind of movies do you like?

What sign of the zodiac are you?

What do you like about your job? What don't you like about it?

Where did you grow up? What are your favorite memories?

What was your major in school? What do you enjoy learning about the most, now that you're out of school?

There are also questions about lifestyles and responsibilities:

What would your ideal house look like? Where do you want to live?

Do you have pets? What kind and how many?

Do you pile things up, or do you have a place for everything and keep everything in its place?

What is your favorite kind of food? Do you have any dietary restrictions?

Then there are the questions that reveal our deep values:

What are your spiritual beliefs?

Where do you go to find tranquillity, solitude, or a connection to a Higher Power?

Are you happy with your health? What are your favorite ways to maintain or improve it?

Who are your closest friends, and why?

What's your family like? Are you close to them?

How do you see yourself in the future?

In *Intellectual Foreplay,* you'll also find questions that reveal some very important realities that can deeply impact a relationship:

What do you respect about yourself? Do you like who you are?

What is your religion? Will you marry outside your religion?

Are you, or have you ever been, in trouble with the law?

Do you consider yourself to be an honest person?

Do you use drugs?

How do you feel about marriage and monogamy?

Do you want to have children?

Do you practice safe sex, and have you recently been tested for HIV or other sexually transmitted diseases?

Most of us have had the experience of discovering something about someone we're close to and saying, "You never told me that!" only to hear the reply, "You never asked." Information may not have been concealed from us, but our friends or partners may simply have not thought the information important or worth sharing until the topic came up naturally. Asking questions is a great way to learn and to initiate deeper conversations. Asking doesn't replace intuition, attraction, or simple observation, but rather works in combination with them. The answers you receive to the questions in this book and your responses to those answers will raise your level of awareness about what you want, what you're getting, and what is important to you. Just reading through these questions will draw your attention toward areas in your relationship and in yourself that may require some attention or that deserve more respect.

The reason they say "love is blind" is that when we are infatuated, needy, wanting, and hoping, we tend to dismiss what we see. The aim of this book is to assist you in really seeing and hearing your partner and getting a feeling for your relationship. Then, with a conscious awareness of both partners' likes, dislikes, preferences, values, beliefs, habits, traditions, level of flexibility, respect, and honesty, you can make an intentional decision to take into your life those ways of being, or to turn away from them. You *choose* your relationship. It doesn't just happen to you. You are a responsible, aware person choosing a life partner *and* all the things that come with that person. As Steven beautifully put it in the courtship stage of our relationship, "In the past, I've gone in with my eyes closed, seeing only what I wanted to see, and things didn't work out. This time, I'm going in seeing everything, and I want what I see."

Getting the Most Out of This Book

As you look through *Intellectual Foreplay,* you'll find that the book is divided into eight major sections. Part One, "Using Your Head and Your Heart," discusses the nuts and bolts of *Intellectual Foreplay* and shows you how to get the most out of this process. Here you will learn how to approach *Intellectual Foreplay* with a partner, what to do with the answers you receive, and how to make it fun for both of you! It is very important that you read Part One before jumping into the sections that list questions. The tools provided in Part One will make handling the information in the rest of the book much easier and the process much more meaningful, rather than just entertaining.

Parts Two through Six are where you will find the questions to explore with a partner. They have been organized into useful categories that explore different aspect of your partner's (and your own) life and character. These categories, or chapters, are further organized around broader questions: Who are you, where did you come from, where are you going, can we live together, and where are *we* going?

These questions, and the order of the chapters in the book, are meant to serve as guidelines for you; there is no need to proceed rigidly through the sequence of questions in the order they're presented here. Choose the sequence that best fits your and your partner's comfort level with the topics and the extent to which your relationship has already developed. But one word of warning: we suggest that you avoid exploring the sex chapter (which falls at the end of the book) with a potential partner until you have read the rest of the book, or, at the very least, Part One. Think of the rest of the book as *foreplay*—it will make the sex chapter (and your relationship) better if you go though the book first!

Part Seven, "Can We Evolve Together?" contains the concluding chapters, "Questions to Ask Yourself" and "Bringing Out the Elation in rELATIONships." These chapters will guide you through the process of getting clear about whether you and your partner should be together, and if so, maintaining peace within your relationship and keeping your love alive. Elation, or joy, is an important component of healthy relationships, and it is yours for the creating.

Intellectual Foreplay Isn't Only for Lovers

Whether you are currently in a relationship or not, whether you're newly involved or celebrating your fiftieth anniversary, there are benefits and rewards to be reaped from exploring *Intellectual Foreplay.* If you are looking for a relationship, it will enhance your vision of what you want. If you are dating, it will provide food for thought, discussion, and discovery during a dinner date. If you are in love and contemplating a serious commitment, it will enhance your knowledge of yourself and your partner and assist you in keeping your eyes fully open as you become more deeply involved. If you are already committed to each other, *Intellectual Foreplay* will assist you in exploring or re-negotiating your relationship at a deeper level. Even your relationship with yourself can improve through the use of this book, as *Intellectual Foreplay* brings about greater self-clarity, awareness, and understanding. *Intellectual Foreplay* can even be used to select roommates and business partners, or to inspire a conversation with your family and friends.

What this book is not is a manual for digging up private or destructive details of each other's past. The criterion for every question selected was, "Is this a purposeful, relevant question to ask?" The questions are also intended to serve as a springboard, stimulating conversation and helping you to develop your own unique set of questions.

You'll note that the term "partner" is used throughout *Intellectual Foreplay* to refer to whomever you're currently considering a relationship with or already seeing. On one level, it is a generic term meaning friend, boyfriend, girlfriend, roommate, husband, wife, or fiancé, but it is also intended to include gay partners and other alternative relationships. The questions in this book are applicable to all human relationships.

On a deeper level, the term "partner" is used because often we forget, when negotiating a relationship, that we are "partners." We are on the same side. We are not in opposition or competition. Ideally, we are a supportive team assisting each other in the journey of life. Remembering that we are *partners* can shift our attitude toward the other person and the relationship, helping us to realize that people don't generally choose to be in partnerships unless they feel that their lives will be enhanced in some way.

Interestingly, "partner" is derived from the word "part," which means "a portion or division of the whole." As partners, we get a sense of both— we are separate and yet a necessary complement to a bigger whole. *Webster's* defines "partner" as "1) One who has a share or part in anything with another or others; a sharer; a participator; a partaker; an associate. 2) One who is associated with one or more persons in the same business and shares with them its profits and risks; a member of a partnership. 3) Either of two persons dancing together. 4) Either or any one of the players on the same side or team. 5) A husband and wife." If we keep these definitions clear in our minds, it is bound to lead to a healthier relationship. The essence of partnership is support, shared risk and gain, teamwork, being friends.

One additional note on language: throughout this book, you will see the words "they," "them," and "their" instead of "he/she," "him/her," and "his/hers." While we acknowledge that it is grammatically incorrect to use plural pronouns when referring to a singular person, it just seemed too cumbersome to do it any other way. Until the language includes a nongendered word that represents both males and females, this will have to suffice. We hope that it is not offensive to the English major within you.

✳

PART ONE

Using Your Head and Your Heart

HOW TO ENGAGE IN
INTELLECTUAL FOREPLAY

MAKING THE RIGHT CHOICE
AND BEING THE RIGHT CHOICE

LOVERS: TO BE OR NOT TO BE?—
MAKING YOUR DECISION

CHAPTER ONE

How to Engage in Intellectual Foreplay

tephanie, a woman in her late twenties, decided she was ready to "settle down." The only challenge was that she wasn't in a relationship. After getting a copy of *Intellectual Foreplay,* she realized that the best way to start looking for "the one" was to go through the process of getting to know herself better and figuring out what she wanted in a partner. She began answering the book's questions, and she shared with us how much she learned about herself. She also admitted that answering the questions honestly, even to herself, wasn't always easy.

As she was going through the book, Stephanie also began interviewing for a new roommate. Figuring that she would use this opportunity to practice, she pulled questions from *Intellectual Foreplay* that were applicable to a roommate situation, and she asked prospective roommates questions that explored whether they could live together. *Intellectual Foreplay* served as an excellent tool for finding someone with whom she could easily share a household.

Later, when Stephanie met a man she was interested in, she selected several questions from *Intellectual Foreplay* and gently wove them into the conversation on their first few dates. When that went well, she showed the book to the man she was dating, Patrick, and honestly explained that she was interested in really getting to know her partner this time around. They then took turns picking the categories and the questions, often bringing out the book instead of turning on the television. Sometimes they made a game of it, using the book with friends at parties, and other times they took it slowly and seriously as they explored their individual and mutual perspectives.

Fortunately, Stephanie approached using *Intellectual Foreplay* in a way that made it fun and comfortable for Patrick to participate. Other people have reported to us that their partners got overwhelmed at the prospect of being interviewed or having to "measure up." How you approach using this book and your mindset as you use it will make all the difference in the world. Having a clear understanding of how *Intellectual Foreplay* is organized and the various methods of using it will help you introduce it to a partner with ease and grace.

As we pointed out in the Introduction, this part of the book provides the conceptual tools that are necessary for making sense of the information you'll receive as you explore *Intellectual Foreplay* with a partner. It is here that you will discover how to approach the subject with a partner and gain an understanding of what to do with the answers after you've asked the questions. You will also find exercises interspersed throughout the book that are designed to help you focus on your personal goals and values, and those of your partner. These have been titled "Foreplay" because they will be more beneficial to you if they are done *first,* before you explore the other questions with a partner. If you take a few minutes to do each exercise, you'll find them to be an excellent reference point to return to as you work your way through *Intellectual Foreplay*—and your life!

In Parts Two through Six of this book, you will find questions to answer yourself and to explore with a partner. Before you start, take some time to familiarize yourself with the topic areas and questions. In the table of contents, you'll see that the questions have been divided into categories that are intended to guide you through the book. The chapters are organized around various topics—romance, values, health, money—and are arranged in a sequence similar to the one you might naturally encounter in a relationship (although this sequence will vary from couple to couple). Remember that *Intellectual Foreplay* is meant as a guide, not an instruction manual. There are no rules when it comes to relationships, as everyone is different. Simply use your best judgment. Your comfort with the topics will depend greatly on how long you have been in the relationship, so be sensitive to your particular situation and skip around in the book as you see fit.

Within each of these chapters, we've subdivided the questions still further: you'll find "Questions to Ask Each Partner," "Questions to Explore as a Couple," "Observations of Your Partner," and "Self-Observations."

"Questions to Ask Each Partner" are questions designed for each partner to ask the other and to answer themselves. These are questions such as: "What are your attitudes about?" or "How do you like to spend your free time?" The answers will obviously be different for each person. *It is highly recommended that you spend some time answering the questions on your own before asking them of a partner.* Knowing yourself is always a good first step. If your partner would prefer that same opportunity, be sure to give them some time alone with the book to think as well.

Other questions are titled **"Questions to Explore as a Couple."** These are questions that you discuss together and that examine your lifestyle as a couple rather than as individuals. Often, these questions deal with issues that you will need to resolve together, by co-creating a system that works for both of you; for example, "Who makes the decisions about major expenses?" You'll find that some questions may not have an answer, as you haven't yet established a set way of doing certain things. For example, if you do not have children, you may not have yet decided how you want to raise them. These questions are where you get to explore your ideas, and create the situation or answer, together.

There are also observation questions in each of these chapters. Generally, these are divided into "Observations of Your Partner" and "Self-Observations." **"Observations of Your Partner"** are questions designed to encourage each partner to reflect on what they have observed in their partner or in a particular situation. These are questions such as, "Does your partner treat you with respect?" You'll discover that you already know the answers to some of these questions simply from experience with your partner, rather than from their answers to your questions. Reading through and answering the observation questions will bring your existing knowledge and awareness into explicit view.

"Self-Observations" are questions for each partner to ask of themselves to facilitate their self-awareness. These include questions such as, "How do you feel when you are with your partner?" You may opt to share your perceptions and observations with your partner by going through these questions together. Be careful not to make assumptions about your partner without checking them out for accuracy, as your assumptions may be off base. Asking your partner about your perceptions will certainly shine some light on the topic at hand.

Part Seven contains a chapter called "Questions to Ask Yourself." Much like the observation questions in each preceding chapter, this chapter is designed to help you to observe yourself as well as to gain a bird's-eye-view of your relationship and make some very important decisions about it. *Feel free to read this chapter before any of the other question chapters, and then go through it again at the end.* Your answers to these questions may reveal to you an innate knowledge about your relationship's likelihood of success, and may spare you a lot of time with the wrong partner.

You may wish to record your and your partner's answers, by either taking notes or using a tape recorder. We've provided some space for you to write answers or notes directly in the book, but this is limited, and you may wish to keep a pad of paper or a notebook handy when you go through the questions with a partner.

When to Ask the Questions

How you use this book will depend on where you are now, in terms of a relationship. **If you are not yet involved with someone,** the book will act as a tool for you to clarify your needs, values, preferences, expectations, and desires for a happy, healthy relationship. You can even use the questions as journal topics for your own self-exploration. Answering these questions can help you to improve your relationship with yourself, enhancing self-clarity, understanding, and awareness. Thus, you can become your own partner in life. When we are whole and complete alone, we tend to have more to offer another in the creation of a healthy relationship. We become less needy. After answering the questions yourself, you will also have an increased awareness of what matters to you and what does not. Knowing what's important to you will assist you in recognizing a suitable partner.

If you are simply looking for a roommate or housemate, with no intimate relationship, this book will assist you in exploring many practical questions aimed at discovering your level of compatibility in sharing a household. Look at the chapters on "Household Responsibilities and Habits," "Bathroom," and even "Entertainment, Sports, and Hobbies." The volume of a roommate's music or how often they want the television on will surely affect you if you are trying to study or if you prefer a quiet household.

If you are a part of the dating world, this book will assist you in clarifying your needs and wants and assessing your compatibility with a prospective partner. Knowing what to talk about and keeping a conversation alive on a date are not always easy. The topics and the questions in this book will make it easier for you to carry on an interesting and informative conversation on a date, even when the book isn't with you. While we were still compiling this book, our friend Lee, a single man in his forties, showed up at our door at six-thirty one morning, asking for "just one page" to help him through a date he had that day. Another young man, Eric, called and said, "Come on, Eve, I'm a dating machine, and I *need* that book!" While on the one hand it seemed funny to need that kind of help, we needed it, too, when we were getting to know each other.

Tom, in his thirties, reported that he was very shy and had dated very little. After going through a dating class in which *Intellectual Foreplay* was mandatory reading, he now always takes the book with him on dates because it provides security, helping him whenever he doesn't know what to talk about.

Although you may not feel comfortable, at the initial dating level, bringing up *all* the questions in this book, the answers to questions on basic values will give you plenty of information with which to decide whether to pursue a next date or relationship. Be selective about what you ask early in the dating process; some questions are definitely inappropriate for a first date, while others will spur you on to a second lively evening of discussion.

Use your best judgment about what is appropriate to ask early in a relationship and what is not. In most cases, weddings and planning a family aren't likely candidates for first-date discussions. However, if they come up naturally or seem appropriate in the context of the conversation, you could explore your prospective partner's interest in these areas early on. There may even be certain things that you need to find out on the first date—or even *before* the first date—in order to determine whether you want to consider the get-together a "date" or "meeting a friend." For example, some people first want to ask about a potential partner's religion; if it isn't a match, it isn't a date.

Your level of comfort in discussing the topics with a partner will vary depending on how long you have known each other. While self-esteem is the first category you should explore *with yourself* (see Chapter Four), some of the questions on this topic may be too intense to explore in the early stages of getting to know a partner, other than through silent observation. We recommend that you skip around and explore the lighter subjects, such as "Entertainment, Sports, and Hobbies," at the beginning stages of dating and then move into more challenging topics as you become more comfortable with each other. It is a wise approach to read through the more serious topics on your own, determine what is of importance to you, and keep it low key until you are ready to talk about those subjects. Remember, Steven and I engaged in this process for over five months through telephone calls and then continued in person when I moved to Maui. The idea isn't to get through the whole book quickly.

Start by generating your own list of essential questions to ask a prospective partner. What do you think you should ask someone before you get seriously involved? Use a separate piece of paper.

A word of warning: We mentioned earlier that you should resist the impulse to go directly to the Sex chapter and start there. Some people skip immediately to the "Sex" chapter because it "gives them permission" to discuss topics that they might not otherwise feel comfortable bringing up. This chapter is at the *end* of the book for a good reason. By going directly to the sex questions and establishing this level of intimacy prematurely, you may end up climbing in bed together before true compatibility has been established. This is the very phenomenon this book was written to avoid. Another consideration is that you may not want to reveal certain information about yourself if you haven't established the trust and shared values that come from discussing the other topics first. If you and your partner are looking for a lasting relationship and cannot get through the self-esteem chapter or the chapter on morals and ethics together before turning to the sex chapter, you aren't ready to have sex.

The **"we're in love; where do we go from here?" stage** is also an ideal time for using this book. This critical point, when you have established definite interest and are asking yourselves whether this is *the* relationship, is a prime time to get out this book and explore all of the questions within it.

Communication is a critical ingredient in a healthy relationship. Discovering, early in the dating process, your potential partner's ability to communicate openly and honestly can save you a lot of frustration, pain, and lamenting. Pay attention if your partner only gives "yes or no" answers or brief, vague nonanswers. Pay attention, too, if your partner hands you a list of questions and just wants you to write down all your answers. Remember, communication is what this is all about. Unless your partner is hearing impaired, the process of *Intellectual Foreplay* should include speaking *and* listening!

If you are already in a committed relationship, you will still find this book useful. All of its questions came from people's experiences in previous or present relationships. When they explored these questions with their partners, new areas of discussion came to light; many of them discovered implicit agreements or unconscious patterns in their relationships. Discussing these questions provided a safe venue for re-examining certain aspects of their relationships, their areas of contentment, joy, resentment, and frustration. *Intellectual Foreplay* will help you look at what works, see why it works, and find out what doesn't work and if anything can be done about it.

The questions are meant to facilitate communication about important philosophical and practical topics that can enhance or interfere with a relationship. People going through divorce, a break-up, or a stressful relationship often feel like victims, as though they are finding out about their partner's beliefs and behaviors for the first time. While people do change over the years—interests change, hobbies change, etc.—the basic social, moral, and behavioral structure of a person's way of being in a relationship is often evident from the very beginning. The best way to avoid being a "victim" is to know these things about your partner from the very start.

How to Ask the Questions

There are many possible ways to introduce *Intellectual Foreplay* to a partner. Some prefer the "Hey, check out this book I found!" approach. This is a direct and simple way of sharing the concept with a partner without saying, "Hi, sit down. I have a few thousand questions to ask you." Others prefer to familiarize themselves with the questions, introducing them into a conversation without bringing out the book until a later date, so to speak. Feel free to rephrase the questions to make them more comfortable to you. While the book may ask a specific question about your partner's past, such as, "Describe your life and your major life events," your style may simply be to ask, "So, what's your story?" Participating in *Intellectual Foreplay* with a partner is meant to be fun and full of discovery. Explore your own personal style while being conscious of how you may come across to your partner.

Asking questions can open the door to hours of lively discussion and discovery; however, that won't happen if your partner feels interrogated. *Intellectual Foreplay is not an interview or intensive exam; it is about the process of getting to know each other.* The questions are to be asked of *each* partner; one partner shouldn't do all the asking while the other does all the answering. Be aware that many people have been asked questions only when someone was checking on them or trying to catch them doing something wrong. Consequently, when being asked questions, they may automatically get defensive or feel intimidated. Keep it light for starters, or you'll scare people away. Approach the questions playfully, as a conversation or a game of personalized "Trivial Pursuit," and everyone will be more comfortable. An excellent approach is to show a potential partner the book, simply saying, "I found this great tool for helping people get to know each other better and I want share it with you." Let them look at it; then bring up a question you want to discuss *and answer it yourself* before expecting your partner to answer. By doing this, you avoid the feeling of interrogation by modeling your willingness to share yourself.

Another approach is to let your partner pick the question categories. The choice of categories in itself is information. While one person may immediately turn to the chapter on "Sex," which tells you what is on their mind, another may turn to "Religion and Spirituality." *Everything is information.*

A fun option is to open the book at random and see what you get. By doing this, you may find that you're more comfortable with the questions because neither of you chose them. This can break the ice of embarrassment over certain questions or categories while you are building trust.

One couple, Lindsey and Mark, had fun using the book and learning about each other by taking on different characters or personas while answering. First, Mark took on the role of "the bad boyfriend," and then he answered as "the new-age boyfriend." Then Lindsey did "the girlfriend who only wants ten kids and doesn't care with who" and the "spoiled princess." It led to hours of laughing while they both learned a lot about each other's personalities and beliefs. They were then able to transition into answering honestly from their own primary personality.

It is important to remember that you're not asking questions to find out what's "wrong" with the other person—or yourself—but simply to find out *who the other person is.* The questions are purely for looking at *what is*—for discovering the reality of your partner's character and the potential of the relationship. There are no right or wrong answers. There are, however, answers in alignment with your own answers. There are answers in alignment with your goals and desires. There are answers in alignment with your lifestyle. *And there are answers that are not in alignment.* Take them all as information. Assess what is of importance to you and file the rest. You'll find exercises in Chapter Two that are designed to help you gain clarity about your goals and values, so that you'll be able to recognize when a partner's answers are in alignment with your own. Take the time to do them before you ask the questions of a partner; thus you'll be able to refer back to them as guideposts for your decision-making process.

As you proceed through the question chapters of *Intellectual Foreplay* with a partner, develop your own mutual style for asking and answering. There really isn't a "right" or "wrong" way to do it. You may choose to have one person ask the other questions that interest them one evening, and then, the next time you get together, switch and have the other person ask. You may wish to alternate back and forth on each question. When Steven and I were in the midst of *Intellectual Foreplay,* if he asked the question, I would answer, and when I was finished, I would ask him the same question.

Imagine several different ways to engage a partner in Intellectual Foreplay that would feel natural and comfortable to you, and write them down. What might you say? Would you show them the book or just prepare some questions? In what different ways might you use it—as an icebreaker at parties, on long drives with the family . . . ? Practicing Intellectual Foreplay makes engaging in it easier.

If you have just met someone and are trying to determine whether to go on a date, go through the book and, after getting very clear on what is important to you, select a handful of questions that will address those issues. For instance, if you are a strict vegetarian and absolutely know that you will not date someone who eats meat, that would be a good starting point for discussion in a pre-date phone call. Remember, this process is not intended for finding fault with the other person, but simply to discover compatibility. If you are not aligned on an issue that you are uncompromising on, spare yourself the anguish of beginning a relationship. (On the other hand, if everything else looks like a perfect match, you may want to examine whether you can stay strong in your convictions and beliefs without having to control your partner's way of living. (Chapter Three will address this further.)

You do not need to go sequentially through the categories or answer the questions in any particular order. Make this fun, and start with the questions that are of primary interest to you both. Keep in mind that not all the questions are important to everybody and therefore some may not need to be asked; however, all the questions came from people who found these topics to be issues in their relationships. Therefore, don't dismiss or take for granted any of the questions unless you are positive that they won't be a concern or issue to you or your partner. Often the only way to know is to go ahead and ask. You may find that some seemingly unimportant topics prove to be important to your partner.

Just as not all the questions are appropriate at all stages in a relationship, not all times of the day or periods of a person's life are appropriate for intensive discussions. When a person is extremely tired, just waking up or falling asleep, stressed or overworked, it isn't wise to try to initiate a deep and meaningful conversation. At the same time, if you find that your partner is *always* too stressed or tired for a meaningful conversation, take that as information. *What you see is what you get!* Will you be happy in a relationship with someone who is never available to you at a deeper level of communication?

Everything Is Information—Listen!

Intellectual Foreplay is not the adult version of "Truth or Dare." *Don't ask anything you don't want to know the answer to, but do pay attention to the areas you avoid, because it is often under avoidance that issues and problems hide.* Only answer what you are willing to answer, but again, pay attention to the areas you have difficulty discussing. Even a refusal to discuss a topic is information for your increased knowledge and awareness. Watch for patterns in your and your partner's discomfort.

Susan, a thirty-eight-year-old divorced woman, found a copy of *Intellectual Foreplay* on her new boyfriend's coffee table. She immediately borrowed it, taking it home in the hope of discovering the secret to avoiding the same mistakes she had made before. After a couple of days of going through the book, she called us for two reasons. One, she wanted to thank us for creating a tool to guide her through the challenges of developing new relationships. Two, she wanted to share a concern. She knew she was going to have to return the book. She exclaimed, "I don't want him to ask me about my past. I want to take a big black marker pen and cross out some of the questions before I give the book back!"

Remember, everything is information. Susan was inadvertently displaying a potential problem for the relationship on many levels. First, she was sharing a lack of self-esteem through her shame or discomfort over the truth about herself. She was also unconsciously admitting a lack of trust in her partner's ability to be understanding and forgiving. Unwillingness to face the truth about oneself is a sign of unresolved issues. Regardless of whether Susan ever chooses to share her past with her partner, it would serve her well to take a careful look at her concerns and, depending on what they are, work on either accepting those qualities in herself or changing them. These issues, when not dealt with, are often the very critters that come back and bite us later.

When we are infatuated with someone or excited about a new love, it is easy to dismiss things as unimportant. Do your best to stay absolutely clear about what you believe in and what you need to be happy. At the same time, remember that you will likely never find someone who answers all the questions in exactly the same way you do. Therefore, the objective is not to find perfectly matching answers, but rather to gain a total awareness of the situation, the matches and the mismatches, so that you can make a conscious choice about the relationship, knowing what you are choosing. *Finding someone who answers in a way that you respect and can joyfully live with is the objective.*

Really listen to what your partner tells you about himself or herself in the beginning of a relationship. When someone says, "I'm not ready for a relationship," or "I don't have time for a relationship," or "Because of my religion, I'm not sure if this will work," or "I really like you, but I'm not looking for something serious," or "I'm too selfish to be good to you in a relationship right now," *believe them!* If you do not, as you struggle through the relationship later, you will undoubtedly find that they told you the truth in the first place. If you want to make the right choice, it is imperative that you do not only hear what you want to hear in the early stages of a relationship. Listen to the information that you are given from the start, and if you don't want to hear it, pay attention to why not.

On the other hand, if you are the one making these relationship-limiting statements, it is important to ask yourself why you are allowing the relationship to develop if these conditions exist. Often these statements are excuses to avoid getting involved and an attempt not to hurt the other person's feelings. Other times, they indicate fear. If you hear these statements, be cautious. If you make these statements, do some more self-exploration before entering into a relationship.

If you go into a relationship with full awareness of what you're getting into, you'll be less likely to find yourself, years into the relationship, saying, "If only I'd known!" Unfortunately, you may find yourself saying, even after asking and discussing all the questions in this book, "If only I'd *paid attention*." This means paying full attention not only to what the other person says, to how *they* react to questions and what they avoid and embrace, but also to how *you* answer the questions, how you react to the questions and to your partner's answers, what you avoid, pretend not to notice, and embrace.

One way of monitoring your own reactions is to pay close attention to your body during the conversations. In Gestalt therapy, clients and therapists are taught to become aware of the sensations in their own bodies and to use those sensations as information about what is happening in a situation. Use your body as a tool. If you feel a knot in your stomach when you're asked a question or when you hear an answer, pay attention to that feeling. What is it telling you? If you feel joyful about an answer, pay attention to that feeling; it is telling you something about what you value and what you expect. If you feel like crying when discussing certain topics, notice. If you find yourself slumped over with the weight of the world on your shoulders during a discussion, pay attention. If you find yourself bored and yawning throughout the discussion, pay attention. If you notice yourself sitting on the edge of your seat, intrigued, fascinated, and laughing, take it in as information. Don't let these clues go by unnoticed. Our bodies are glorious perceivers of information, and they do not lie to us. It is an art to tune in and be aware. It is well worth your time to become conscious of these messages.

Start Smart

Wendee Mason, founder and instructor of Date Smart Seminars in southern California, has been using *Intellectual Foreplay* as required reading in her classes for several years. She instructs the students to go through the book carefully and pull out their "top twenty non-negotiable questions" to discuss on what she calls the "pre-date," which is intended to determine if the other person qualifies for a real date. Pre-dates are held during the day in a neutral place; for example, you might have lunch in a restaurant to which you both drove separately. She further explains that if the other person isn't a match on those first twenty questions, you should save yourself the time and energy of continuing in a relationship with that partner.

One student in Wendee's dating class, Steve ("her" Steve is not to be confused with "my" Steven), took her words very seriously and asked Wendee herself out on a pre-date of walking her dog on the beach. She agreed, and as they walked she saw him referring to some index cards he held in the palm of his hand. It was then that she realized that he had his top twenty questions prepared and was now going through them with *her!* The next four or five times they got together, he did the same thing—pulling the next twenty most important questions out of *Intellectual Foreplay,* putting them on index cards, and bringing them along for discussion.

At this point she told him that if he wanted to get serious, they needed to go through the whole book—cover to cover. She then added some incentive by letting him know that she wouldn't go to bed with him until they finished. Soon into the chapters, they discovered that they had different communication styles that needed to be honored. Steve preferred to think about his answers, write them down, and then discuss them, but she preferred to talk with him about her answers on the spot. They also determined that they wanted to record their answers for future reference. They agreed that every day he would write his answers down and mail them to her on index cards (he is a mailman), and she would discuss her answers with him in person, recording them on tape at the same time. Every day for the next ninety days, Wendee received twenty index cards in the mail with Steve's answers written on them, and every time they got together, she answered questions, recording her answers for him. They went through the entire book! Between the two of them, they spent half a year getting to know each other in this way. They have now been together for several years and claim their relationship to be the most secure, solid bond either of them has experienced.

When I interviewed Steve, he shared that when he and Wendee went on dates, they brought along the tape recorder. Once, after dinner, they found a spot along the shoreline where a streetlight lit up a bench and the crashing waves. They spent hours watching the ocean, discussing and recording the questions in the book. Not only was it a fun and lively date, but it was in a romantic setting as well.

You may also wish to record your answers. Wendee points out that it provides a wonderful reference that you can use to remind yourself why you fell in love with your partner in the first place. However, it can also provide "proof" of what you were told, which could be misused later in a relationship. Be careful of how you use this tool. It isn't meant to trap people into one way of thinking for the rest of their lives. You are always free to change your mind; just be clear and communicate about it. Use your own judgment and discover your very own style for using *Intellectual Foreplay*.

As you go through the questions in this book, select what you consider to be your top twenty "non-negotiable" questions and record them on a separate piece of paper or on index cards. Take the time to answer them yourself and consider what these questions reveal that is of importance to you, before you ask these questions of your partner.

Just as Wendee and Steve found comfortable places to engage in Intellectual Foreplay—the beach, over dinner at a restaurant—imagine some possible places and times for you and a partner to comfortably explore the answers. What is the perfect setting for you to engage in Intellectual Foreplay? When do opportunities for sharing emerge naturally—driving in the car, talking on the telephone . . . ? List your ideas on a separate piece of paper.

CHAPTER TWO

Making the
Right Choice and
Being the Right Choice

ome people have suggested that I should have listed the "right" answers in this book, not just questions. If I were to include what I think are the "right" answers, you would all end up with perfect partners for *me*, rather than the right choice for you! *Intellectual Foreplay* is a guide for approaching important questions in a relationship, but you must be the one to determine what is the right answer for you. Be specific. Do you want to go to parties all of the time or stay home? Do you want an active, outdoors lifestyle or do you prefer reading books or watching television? There are no "right answers" to any of the questions in the book; there are, however, answers that indicate a right choice for *you*.

As Steven and I were practicing *Intellectual Foreplay*, getting to know each other over the phone, both of us were concerned with the *other* person's answers to our questions. One night it suddenly dawned on me that what I said—*my answers*—were just as important as his. This may seem obvious, but in the midst of my effort to determine if he was a right choice for me, I didn't think about *whether I was a right choice for him*.

What is the right choice? A right choice is entirely an individual decision. "Right" is a person who has the qualities that you feel are important, and the only way to know what you find important is to look at your own values and beliefs and ask yourself what really matters to you. So getting to know your partner is only one aspect of *Intellectual Foreplay.* The other, equally critical, aspect is *getting to know yourself, and making conscious decisions about who you are and how you want to be.*

Discover Your Witness Self

In order to know whether you are the right choice for someone else, it is important to first take a look at who you are and how you show up in the world, and assess how you feel about yourself. In order to do this, you must discover, and access, your Witness Self. This is a process of self-observation in which you allow yourself to just watch *yourself.* Simply ask, "What am I doing now?" or "How am I feeling now?" and pay attention to the answers. It is a bit like taking a snapshot of yourself in the moment.

Sometimes, when I discuss a situation with Steven, I hear a voice in the back of my mind that says, "My tone of voice sounds angry right now." My Witness Self is observing my behavior and feelings and giving me feedback. With this awareness, I can self-adjust. For example, I can alter my tone of voice to communicate in a more respectful way. If I didn't observe myself, I would unconsciously continue in a nagging or angry tone, and my message would get lost in the unpleasant delivery. When you learn the art of self-observation, the perspective of your Witness Self, which is a calm and centered place within yourself, becomes an easily accessible state of awareness. Then, if you don't like how you are feeling or responding to a situation, you can make a choice to self-adjust. Taking several deep breaths and consciously breathing out the tension are very helpful for aligning with the Witness Self.

 Stop periodically throughout the day and consciously tune in to how you're feeling. As you go through Intellectual Foreplay, observe yourself as you read. What feelings and emotions do certain topics and questions evoke? How do you feel right now?

Fritz Perls, the originator and developer of Gestalt therapy, broke the word "responsibility" into two parts: **response-ability,** the *ability* to *respond,* to choose our thoughts, feelings, and emotions in different situations. It is crucial that we develop our response-ability to enable ourselves to create healthy outcomes in our lives. Self-observation is required in order to be able to choose responses that are in alignment with our goals. Without self-observation, we float through life on automatic pilot, not realizing that we are very capable of controlling the direction of our lives. When we are unconscious about what we do, we cannot change. Through self-observation, we become aware. Then, we are in the powerful position of making new choices, of being response-able.

When we observe ourselves, we recognize that there is a part of ourselves, the witness, that is not involved in the drama of our emotions. It simply watches, while remaining strong and resourceful. When we recognize that this aspect of our being, our Witness Self, is not buying into the drama of our ego-self, we realize that we can *choose* to identify with this witness state rather than with our emotions. We can choose to create drama, or we can choose not to. As in the example above, by observing myself as angry, I recognize that the part of myself that does the observing—the Witness Self—is *not* angry. It doesn't *feel* the emotion; it merely *observes* the anger. By recognizing that the witness isn't caught up in the emotion, I can then make a choice to identify with this strong and centered aspect of my being rather than with the anger. From the perspective of the witness, I am far more likely to respond with choices and statements that are wise than with choices ruled by flaring emotions.

Just as discovering your Witness Self can help you observe your *own* actions without judgment, it is also possible to identify with your Witness Self and simply observe your *partner's* actions without judgment. It is a wonderful experience to be with someone through their emotional expressions and feel no judgment or need to control, and it is also a wonderful feeling to be able to be yourself with your partner without criticism or seeking their approval. Discovering your Witness Self is crucial for this to happen.

If you find, as you look at the questions in this book, that you aren't comfortable with who you are, you won't be able to believe that someone else is comfortable with who you are. *Satisfaction in the relationship has to start with satisfaction with yourself.* By going through the questions and exploring your own answers before you share them with a partner, you will enhance your relationship with yourself. If you're practicing self-observation and you don't like what you see, take it as a magnificent gift of insight and start making the changes that you deem necessary. Your own personal happiness is at stake here, whether or not you are ever in a relationship with someone else. Your relationship with yourself is the first place to start.

My friend Alex had a preview copy of *Intellectual Foreplay*'s manuscript on her living-room table. When she came home one day, she found her friend Beth reading it and crying. When Alex asked Beth what she was so upset about, Beth explained that she had come across a question that asked about successes and accomplishments. Alex, still confused by the display of tears, asked, "So?" Beth began crying anew as she answered, "I don't have any!" Although of course that was not true, as it is not possible for someone to make it to her thirties with absolutely no successes, what was true was that Beth didn't feel good about her life. While it wasn't a comfortable discovery, it was a blessing because now she could begin to do something about it— whether by creating successes or by identifying existing ones. When we are unconscious, it isn't possible for us to make the necessary changes to be joyful and esteemed. *Through self-observation, we gain awareness, and with awareness we can begin the process of transformation.*

Examine Your Values

An excellent starting point for *Intellectual Foreplay* is to clarify your own values, whether your intention is to enhance a relationship or to simply gain self-knowledge. Just as it is important that your partner act in alignment with what they say, so is it true for you. Self-esteem is deeply damaged when we claim that certain beliefs or values are important to us but we do not live in alignment with them. The gap between what we *believe* and what we *do* reflects our self-esteem. The more aligned we are, the better we feel about ourselves and our lives. The same is true for our relationships. The better aligned our partners' values are with our own, the better we will feel about our relationships.

If you look at this book's table of contents, you'll see that it is basically a list of values. Look them over, add some of your own, and eliminate any that don't stand out as critically important to you. Prioritizing your values will assist you in decision-making should two values come into conflict. For instance, if you are ever in a position of choosing between work, family, or travel, identifying in advance which has the greatest importance to you can reduce some of the conflict.

Brainstorm your list of personal values on a separate piece of paper or put each one on a Post-it (so that you can re-order them). Prioritize the list, identifying the top ten most-important ones. Return to this list over and over again as you go through Intellectual Foreplay. These are your core values, and they will guide you toward finding the right partner and being the right partner as you look for someone who shares similar values.

When I did this exercise for the first time, I found myself humming a song all the while I was writing. My initial list included: 1) service to God; 2) appreciation; 3) kindness, compassion, and love; 4) honesty, trust, and sincerity; 5) health and strength; 6) personal and spiritual growth; 7) creativity and artistic expression; 8) knowledge and intellectual growth; 9) beauty, peace, and aesthetics; and, 10) productivity and financial self-sufficiency. As I finished identifying, defining, and prioritizing my list, I began to wonder what the song was that had been going through my head. As I put words to the tune, I realized that it was the Camp Fire Girl Law. (Camp Fire Girls was a club, similar to Girl Scouts.) The words were: "Worship God, seek beauty, give service and knowledge pursue. Be trustworthy ever in all that you do. Hold fast onto health and your work glorify, and you will be happy in the Law of Camp Fire." As I looked down at my journal, I was amazed to see that virtually every one of the values declared in that little song were on my paper.

As you identify your values, consider where you adopted them. Did your family teach you these values? Did television teach you these values? Do you really *honor* them, or have you just unconsciously listed them without commitment? Be sure that the values you list are truly your own and that you are dedicated to living in alignment with them, and then dedicate yourself to doing so. The results will be enhanced self-esteem and greater clarity and focus.

In order to live in alignment with the values that you have chosen, it helps to define what they mean to you. What "service to God" and "appreciation" mean to me may be very different than what they mean to you. Once you are clear about what each value means, then you can actively take steps to live your values. For instance, to me, "appreciation" means having a constant attitude of gratitude, remembering in every moment to be thankful for the blessings that surround me—both those that are obvious and those that are harder to recognize. In order to act in alignment with this value, I literally say, "Thank you" out loud when I get a parking space in a crowded lot, when I find something I have lost, when I sit down to a meal, and even when I encounter a challenge or difficulty. I trust that everything is a blessing, and my task is to see it that way. For me, having a partner who also sees life as a blessing is critically important. It is a non-negotiable item because it is one of my personal core values.

> **How do you live in alignment with your values? After you have identified your values—what is important to you—spend a moment defining what each one means to you. Then, jot down a few different ways that you live in alignment with your values in your daily life—or ways in which you could live in alignment with them.**

One fun way to identify your values is to get a highlighter pen and the personal ads from a newspaper. Go through the ads looking for qualities that you want in your partner and in your life. The joy here is that you aren't looking for one ad, but rather qualities from many listings that together create a composite all your own. You will find that the things you highlight are values or have values embedded in them. Many years ago I was reading through the personals just for fun and found myself "falling in love" with one of the people in the ads. When I stopped for a moment to observe myself, I realized that my yearning was not for a person—as there was no person actually involved—but rather for the experiences and qualities that

I wanted more of in my life. The ad mentioned fires on the beach and sunset walks, in which *romance* and *time in nature* were embedded values. Rather than seeking out the guy who listed them, I chose to seek out opportunities to do those activities more often.

What Is Your Type?

One factor that complicates our ability to make decisions is that we all have preconceived images of what kind of person is our "type" and prejudices about what a person's "type" is, based on visual information. We also have preconceived ideas of how love should feel. We narrow our options by deciding to date only people of a certain race, a certain height, or a certain hair color, or people who must wear a suit to work or have a certain income or level of education; only these people, we believe, are acceptable "partner material." Whatever the criteria, these are all fairly superficial images that can keep us from getting to know people with whom we may have much more meaningful things in common. Images can also lead us to get involved with people whom we later discover are not good choices.

When we meet someone, we often create an image in our heads of who that person is and what a relationship with them would be like. Our expectations, needs, and desires create a fantasy that often doesn't match reality at all. We may fall in love with our own picture of a person rather than with the real person. We may also fall in love with the dream of what we *want* a relationship to be rather than with the reality of the relationship. One man, Tim, tried to hold onto a relationship with his wife because he was in love with the *idea* of being in a happy family: husband, wife, and daughter. However, in all the years of their marriage, reality never matched his picture. She cheated on him repeatedly, and he hadn't been truly happy since they were married. *It is often the illusion or image of what we want a relationship to be that we have the hardest time letting go of—more so than the truth.*

Take a look at your own images or fantasies about a potential partner. What images are you in love with? If you're not sure, again turn to the personal-ads section of the newspaper and circle the ones that appeal to you. Since there is no real face or person attached to these ads, you will see the images you're attracted to developing in your head. It is reasonable and wise to have criteria for a partner, but the point here is to aim for criteria around the issues that are truly important to you, the issues on which you find yourself uncompromising. You might find that all your real criteria are met by someone who has a different physical presentation than you imagined. *Remember the concept of FOURplay, focusing upon mental, emotional, and spiritual values rather than just the physical ones.*

Declare what you want in a partner. For example, "I choose to be with someone who loves animals, who can keep pace with me athletically, who knows how to fix a broken bicycle, who is compassionate and friendly, etc." Be specific! One woman we know asked for "a husband" and got somebody else's! Whom do you imagine to be the "right choice" for you? How has your image of the ideal partner changed over time?

What qualities, experiences, and activities do you yearn for in a rela-tionship—or your life? Using the personal-ads section of the newspa-per, highlight the qualities or activities that you are drawn to and gen-erate a list. How many of those activities can you go ahead and do, regardless of whether you have a partner or not? Which qualities can you develop in yourself? Which ones are mandatory in a partner in order for you to be happy? How does this list compare to your list of values?

Incorporating the above experiences and activities, describe an ideal relationship. If you already have a partner, have them do the same. Compare your description with your partner's, and discover whether you can co-create your relationship in the way you both want it to be.

Refer back to these exercises after going through the rest of the book and see if your answers have changed, or if you need to add to them.

An interesting thing to consider is the fairy-tale idea that there is only one right choice. Many of us held this belief growing up, and perhaps we still do. What if there are many potential right choices? The catch is that each one brings with it a different set of circumstances that must be accept-ed. When considering the idea of "right choice," it is important to recognize that the choice is not just the person, it is also the lifestyle and the lessons to be learned. As annoying as the saying "There are many fish in the sea" can be, it is true that we do have many choices. We may be able to be happy with many different people; however, our goals might not be realized as easily with some people as with others, and with some there may be more inherent difficulties to overcome. When I chose to marry Steven, I also had to accept that he had made his home in Hawaii. Although that's obviously desirable on one hand, it is not always easy to be so far away from the mainland, family, and friends. I chose more than Steven; I chose a way of living. Again, return to your list of values as you go through *Intellectual Foreplay,* and consider how well you will be able to live in alignment with your values if you choose different lifestyles or partners.

As important as developing a clear picture of the "right choice" is developing your idea of the *wrong* choice and then avoiding it. This process is the inverse of the one that you've undertaken. For me, this list would look something like this: I am not willing to be in a relationship with someone who is abusive in any way, including physical abuse, emotional abuse, or substance abuse. I am not willing to be in a relationship with someone who is closed-minded. I am not willing to be with someone who is oblivious to or unappreciative of the many blessings that life has to offer. I am not willing to be with someone who is selfish or lacks compassion for other people.

List the qualities that you are unwilling to accept in a relationship. It is powerful to say, "I am not willing . . ." As you make your list, pay attention to how it feels to make such a strong statement. Are you willing to live in alignment with these convictions?

When you first meet a potential partner, you automatically notice their good qualities, but it is valuable to also pay attention to your concerns or the possible "negatives" of being in a relationship with this person. Compare these concerns with your list of what you're not willing to accept in your life, while at the same time comparing your potential partner's good qualities with what you do want. Unfortunately, the "good stuff," no matter how wonderful, is usually not enough to keep a relationship together if the nature of the "bad stuff" goes against your basic values. Eventually, you may not be able to live happily with the bad stuff, so be aware of it as you enter the relationship.

Oddly enough, when a relationship falls apart, we can often remember early warning signs to which we paid no attention. The ultimate question is: *Why do we try to make a relationship where there should not be one, based on our own criteria?* When we do not feel whole or complete on our own—a lack of self-esteem— we think we need someone else to complete us. We then let the desire to have a relationship push us into creating the wrong one or staying in a bad one.

Seeking Alignment

Once you have your values clearly identified, take a look at your partner's values. While exact matches aren't the point, complementary values are important. What you want to avoid are conflicting values. One couple we know did the exercise below and discovered that although many of their values were the same, they were not listed in the same order. Her highest value was "family," but his was "financial security." This turned out to be an asset. His emphasis on money allowed her the opportunity to concentrate on the family. Thus, there was no problem. However, if family was nowhere to be found on his list and financial security was nowhere on hers, trouble could have begun to brew.

After you've compiled your own list of values and explored what you will and won't accept in a relationship, it's time to talk to your partner about their values. Ask them to write down and prioritize their own list. Compare and discuss your lists. Are they complementary or conflicting?

While it is valuable to pay attention to what your partner literally says when discussing the questions in this book, also listen for the bigger messages— values, belief systems, prejudices, past "baggage," and future goals that are hidden in their way of communicating. Every conversation or interaction supplies information about people and their beliefs, if you pay attention. If your partner or potential partner won't list their values for you to see (take that as information…) but *is* willing to discuss the questions in *Intellectual Foreplay*, look for the questions that will reveal whether their values are in alignment with yours. If exercise, for example, is an important value for you, turn to the chapter on health and explore the questions there. The information will be there in your partner's answers if you look and listen for it. If you listen carefully to a person's words, jokes, comments, and complaints, you will hear patterns emerge that are indicative of deep-rooted beliefs and behaviors and that reveal who they are (feminist or chauvinistic, tolerant or prejudiced, kind or judgmental).

Pay attention, also, to patterns in your and your partner's past relationships. Are one or both of you repeating an old pattern? We (humans) repeat experiences many, many times before we learn the lesson and try something different. By recognizing that we're heading into the same old classroom, we can utilize previous learning and avoid another poor choice before we shut the door and sit down. *One definition of an insane expectation is: "Doing the exact same thing and expecting different results."* Self-observation is necessary in order to recognize and avoid this cycle. Often, all we have to do to stop "doing the exact same thing while expecting different results" is let go of our images and make new, conscious choices.

There's a simple, to-the-point question that you can ask now and that could cut short your need for any of the other questions in this book: *Is my partner a nourishing or toxic person?* The answer may not come in words, but merely in a feeling in your heart or stomach.

A nourishing person is someone who supports your interests and shows consideration and genuine care and concern for you; a person capable of empathy, love, honesty, and understanding; a person with whom you feel good about yourself, your interaction with them, and life in general. Their nourishment is not, however, only felt by you. Nourishing people contribute to society, even by simply living an honest, good life.

A toxic person is someone around whom you never quite feel comfortable about yourself and you never feel truly happy about the way the relationship is going; a person with whom a healthy relationship is very difficult. A toxic person often is stuck in an unskilled manner of communicating needs, e.g., nagging, dishonesty, manipulation, and put-downs. Their "care and concern" may just be well-camouflaged selfishness and manipulation. A toxic person may even be a well-meaning person who has experienced so many negative interactions in their childhood or past that they no longer relate to others in a healthy manner. They may be operating on autopilot, unaware of their ability to respond and make choices. When people are stuck in their needs for approval and control and are not practiced at observing themselves, becoming aware, and making thoughtful decisions, the effect is often toxicity.

Sometimes a person becomes toxic in relationship to someone else, although they may not have been toxic previously. It's much like two chemicals that are neutral on their own, but when mixed cause poisonous fumes. There are people whose styles just plain don't mix. Sometimes toxicity is even contagious, which means that you must choose whom you "mix" with wisely.

An even more important question is: *Which one are you—nourishing or toxic?* Hard as self-analysis may be, if you are a toxic person yourself, it matters not what the other person is. If you are stuck in your need for approval, you will attract people with a need for control. If you are stuck in your need for control, you will attract people with a need for approval. *In order to make a "right choice" in a partner, it is important to be a right choice to your partner.* If you have not done the necessary preparation work to make yourself and your life desirable to *you,* it is unlikely that you or your life will be desirable to someone else.

Happily-Ever-After Always Begins Within

"Happily-ever-after" doesn't mean that you will never encounter difficulties or have challenges to overcome or survive. Rather, it is an approach to living and an approach to loving that is conscious, confident, communicative, and healthy. It means having a sense of responsibility for the life you are creating and the quality of your relationships. Happily-ever-after means that you are happy—sometimes because of your relationship and sometimes in spite of it.

Our relationship with ourselves determines whether we will live happily-ever-after more than our relationships with others do. This is because when we truly love ourselves, we are full. When we are full, we have more to offer—"our cup runneth over," so to speak. When we do not supply ourselves with love, we become needy and expect others to fill us. This creates the potential for tremendous suffering. Not only is it a huge responsibility to make someone else happy, but it is also virtually impossible over time. When we take responsibility for raising our self-esteem and being happy with who we are, we contribute greatly to the quality of our relationships.

A good exercise for raising self-esteem is to *"Be kind to the person you will be tomorrow."* Odd as this sounds, it is simply a matter of looking ahead and handling today the things that will make tomorrow easier. The idea is having consideration for yourself, just as though you were someone else. If you're driving home at night and the car needs gas, rather than waiting until the next day and burdening the self you will be in the morning with an empty tank, fill the tank with gas now. You will love yourself more in the morning. By being continuously considerate of yourself, you will find that life goes easier, you are happier, and you have more joy to share. This applies to being kind to the person you will be years down the line, too. Whether you're considering simple daily tasks such as filling the gas tank or choosing to drink less in honor of the morning after or eating carefully for a healthy future, the concept is the same. The choices you make now will impact *who* you are and *how* you are later. This exercise is also good practice for a relationship, as consideration of the other person is an essential ingredient.

Another way of living to raise your self-esteem and prepare for a relationship is to create in yourself the qualities you're looking for in someone else. *It is not reasonable to expect more from someone else than you expect from yourself.* If you want an honest person who works hard and enjoys the out-of-doors, *be* an honest person who works hard and enjoys the out-of-doors. If you want a spiritual person in your life, be a spiritual person. If you don't want someone who drinks or does drugs, don't drink or do drugs yourself. If you want someone physically fit, become physically fit. The reasons for this are twofold. First, you will satisfy your desires, because you will develop the qualities you're wishing for in your life. Secondly, you will prepare yourself. *You will more likely attract and recognize the kind of person you want when you are that kind of person yourself.*

Along the lines of preparation, take a serious look at your life and see whether you have made room for a partner. Ask, "Is my life attractive to someone else?" We once visited a lonely male friend who had *Playboy* center-folds, posters, and calendars all over his house. I imagined how uncomfortable I would feel if I were his date walking into this environment. We talked with him about making his home welcoming and attractive should he bring home a potential partner. We need to make room for others if we want others in our life. This doesn't mean that we must hide who we are, but rather that we should be the type of person with whom we would want to be in a relationship. Take a look at your surroundings and ask yourself which values you are communicating through them. If you're surrounded with values that don't really matter to you, or if the things you truly find important are not evident, consider ways to remedy the situation.

How would your life be different if you were already in the ideal relationship? Would you do different things with your time? Would you save or plan for the future? Would you take better care of yourself? Would you move to a different part of the world? Would you watch more sunsets? Take more walks? Go out to dinner more often? When I asked a student this question, she replied, "I'd eat brunch every Sunday and then take the dog for a walk on the beach. I'd go to the movies more often. I'd exercise at least four times a week with my partner. I'd try a new restaurant every week." With a little guided self-observation, she was able to see that she didn't have to wait for a partner to incorporate any of those activities into her life. By doing them now, regardless of a partner, she would feel better about her life and enjoy many activities that she was currently missing, and while she was out doing what she loved to do, she might even meet someone who liked to do the same things.

 Make a list of the changes you would make if you were in the ideal relationship, and then incorporate the changes that you can make now into your life—for yourself.

Doing what you love is an excellent way to meet people who also love to do those same things. Regardless of whether you have a partner, you don't have to wait for another person to live the way you want. We can create experiences for ourselves by living in alignment with our values, whether our partner chooses to or not. Who knows, you may find they, too, are waiting for someone else to create the experience for them. *The first step to making the "right choice" is to be your own right choice.*

Process versus Result

A consideration, when contemplating the right choice, is the concept of process versus result. In terms of relationships, focusing on the "process" means concentrating on the *experience* of being together, and focusing on the "result" means concentrating on the *outcome*—happily-ever-after. The reason I mention this is that a long-term relationship may not always be your focus when making a choice. If you look back on the relationships in your life that didn't work out, you can usually identify many good experiences and lessons that you learned during those relationships. Sometimes the long-term success of the relationship is not as important to us as the experience. This is basically the meaning of the old saying "It is better to have loved and lost, than never to have loved at all."

Which you value more, process or result, is often determined by what stage of life you're in and your present goals. If you just want a friend, lover, and/or someone to do things with, it may not matter to you if the relationship works out in the long run; you're likely more interested in the process. If your goal is to get married and have children, you are probably pretty concerned with the result, or outcome, of staying together. Of course, you also care about the quality of the relationship (the process), as one does not necessarily exclude the other, but making the right choice carries a whole new weight if you are process-oriented rather than result-oriented.

 What are your goals for a relationship at this point in your life? What are you ready for right now, and what are you intending to create in the long run? Be honest with yourself. Then, be honest with your partner.

When I was making the decision to marry Steven, I was fearful as I considered the "what if's." *What if* he leaves me, *what if* it doesn't work out, *what if* he's not trustworthy? I came to peace with all these concerns when I realized that it wasn't only Steven whom I needed to trust. I needed to trust God, and *I needed to trust myself.* I needed to trust that I could handle anything that happened and that I would embrace any situation as an opportunity to grow. I needed to trust my ability to respond, rather than worry about the outcome of the situation. Through self-observation, I determined that I wanted to be his wife, regardless of the results. From this place of trust in myself, I was empowered to move forward in the relationship.

You can ask all the questions in the universe and still have that nudging little voice of intuition that tells you this relationship is not the one for you or tells you to embrace the other person fully and allow the relationship to develop. In order to hear that knowing voice within and make a conscientious decision, it is necessary to be silent and listen with your heart. *Focus on the voice of intuition that you hear in peaceful silence, the one grounded in strength.* If the voice is chaotic and weak, it is not the voice of intuition.

SatisfACTION

Everything mentioned previously in this book has focused on helping you gain the awareness necessary for making educated decisions and choices. But there is one very important ingredient that has only been alluded to so far. That is the concept of *action.* It doesn't matter what you know if you are unwilling to take the action required to make use of it. We all know the negative effects of smoking, but are we willing to stop? We all know what we have to do to lose weight and get in shape, but are we willing to do it? We also know when we're involved in a relationship that isn't right for us, but are we willing to make the necessary changes to fix it, accept it, or leave it? Our power dwells in our ability to respond, make a clear choice, and act in alignment with that choice.

Keep this equation in mind:

AWARENESS + ALIGNED ACTION = GROWTH and CHANGE

Action without awareness often results in impulsive, poor choices. If you were to jump out of an airplane without the understanding of how to do it properly, the result would likely be death. On the other hand, awareness without aligned action just results in someone who "should know better." You may take all the skydiving classes in the world, but if you don't take the action that is aligned with that awareness—jumping out of the airplane— you haven't really *learned* how to skydive. We must combine the two in order to create meaningful choices and changes in our lives. If you want satisfaction, you need awareness, and you need to take action.

Intellectual Foreplay is about using your head to make choices that are in alignment with your heart. Each action taken should always pass the "love test." We are referring here to healthy love, not needy, manipulative "love." Healthy love serves the highest good for all involved. To see if your actions pass the "love test," consider these questions: Does this action lead to love? Does this action come from love? Is it purposeful? Is this choice based on respect for myself and all involved? Whenever an action comes from the ego, the need to control, or the need to get approval, it does not come from love. Take the time to stop, watch, catch yourself, and replenish yourself if your thoughts, words and actions do not originate in love.

In a relationship that lasts for years, one guarantee is that circumstances will change. People's goals change, health changes, new interests emerge, new information is introduced that influences our attitudes and beliefs, and, in this day and age, new technology constantly changes the way we do things and use our time. Although exploring the questions in *Intellectual Foreplay* will give you a snapshot of where you and your partner have been and where you both are right now, it doesn't predict the future—for you or them. It does, however, help you to *create* the future through your choices. By knowing each of your basic core values, enhancing your self-esteem, and developing your communication skills, you can create a relationship that is able to deal with changes respectfully and responsibly. By looking at each event as it emerges and choosing actions aligned with your goals and values, together you can create mutually satisfying relationships.

CHAPTER THREE

Lovers: To Be
or Not to Be?

 o you've asked your partner a zillion and one questions. You've found areas of both compatibility and of a total difference in habits, traditions, values, and goals. What do you do now? This chapter will guide you through the process of making sense out of what you discover from engaging in *Intellectual Foreplay*. Read it before you go into the questions, and return to it when you are done.

It seems so complex, at first, as you evaluate the information you've received. This is because, in part, not all information is created equal. Everything has a different weight depending on your value structure, your own answers to the questions, your family background, and your upbringing. Another complication is the conflict between physical attraction and information to the contrary. Your personal level of neediness, vulnerability, and self-esteem also plays a part in your action plan. Also on the playing field are our egos, which are easily bruised and can be quite stubborn.

Relationships trigger our desire to love and be loved. This is all any of us really wants on a core, soul level. When we encounter a conflict in a relationship, one or both of these desires is threatened. Either we feel that our partner disapproves of us, which threatens our sense of being loved, or our own disapproval of them threatens our sense of being loving. Jim Britt points out in *Rings of Truth* that our egos mistake our desire to be loved for a *need for approval* and turn the desire to love into a *need to control*. We then enter into approval-and-control battles with our loved ones that stop us from being able to see viable options and resources that are available to us for remaining loving. When this happens, one or both partners needs to step back, observe the situation, become aware of what is happening, and make choices aligned with the goal of a healthy, loving relationship.

Events, Responses, and Outcomes in Our Relationships

The equation

$$EVENT + RESPONSE = OUTCOME,$$

otherwise referred to as **E + R = O**

is taught by Jack Canfield, a leader in the area of self-esteem and co-author of *Chicken Soup for the Soul*, to help people discover the power they have to create their experiences in life. This equation has a multitude of applications, and it is equally valid applied to relationships. What it essentially means is that though we often do not have control over the events in our lives, we do have control over our *response* to those events. The Event combined with our Response creates the Outcome; thus $E + R = O$. This is a very powerful and empowering message. We do not have control over everything that happens or all the circumstances in which we must operate; however, we do have control over ourselves and can choose how to respond, what to think, feel, say, and do. We are the creators of the outcome. Our power lies in the choice of our response. By taking a moment to observe ourselves and the *events* that we are involved in, and to then choose *responses* to our circumstances that will lead us toward our goals, we create the *outcome* of our lives.

On my thirty-sixth birthday, Steven and I got dressed up and ready to go out to dinner. We stopped at a store on the way, and as we were leaving we passed in front of a small hot-dog concession at the very moment that the worker unhooked her cart from the water outlet on the wall of a building. She did something wrong, causing a blast of water, much like a fire hydrant's, to spray all over us. Since it was such a surprise, it took me a moment to figure out what was going on and get out of the way. Steven and I were both drenched when we met up again on the other side of the wall of water. Still in shock, we stood there for a moment, contemplating our options and discussing what to do. We thought about getting mad (i.e., needing control), but it was my birthday and we didn't want to ruin it by being angry. We thought about demanding some form of compensation, but it was a hot-dog stand and I am a vegetarian. We thought about yelling at the girl for being so stupid, but had she been our daughter, we wouldn't have wanted her to be treated that way for making a mistake. In a sort of surreal way, we filed through our response options, dismissing each for various reasons, before settling on laughing about it, going home to change, and going somewhere else for dinner.

The event was that we had been sprayed with water and gotten soaking wet. After a moment of self-observation, our chosen response was to laugh about it and add it to our lengthy list of funny life experiences. The outcome was a pleasant evening. It was not the event that created the outcome of our evening, but rather how we *chose to respond* to the event. Our power comes in our ability to choose our responses.

In this chapter, I have applied this same concept to the use of *Intellectual Foreplay*. If you plug in the $E + R = O$ equation, your partner's answers to the questions are essentially the E or the event, the "what is." As mentioned earlier, this is the part of the equation over which you have little, if any, power or control. What you do with that information is your response. The event combined with your response is what creates the outcome.

I have identified four pure options in the response category. ("Pure" is explained later.) The options are:

negotiation to change "what is,"

resistance to what is,

acceptance of what is, and

getting out of the equation/relationship or situation.

As you engage in *Intellectual Foreplay*, $E + R = O$ will help you not only in choosing a partner, but also in making choices *within* the relationship that are in alignment with your values and goals. The previous lists that you generated (see Chapter Two) will help guide you in determining when to accept what is and when to get out.

In the context of *Intellectual Foreplay*, E + R = O looks like this:

EVENT ⊕	RESPONSE ⊜	OUTCOME
"What Is"	**1. Negotiation** Attempt to change the "E" or solve the problem.	**A. Change of "E"** **B. No change of "E"** (either result leads you to Response option 2, 3, or 4)
Answers to the questions. Who your partner is; i.e., their behavior, beliefs, attitudes, traditions, habits, values, likes, dislikes, family, past, goals, where they choose to live, what they do for a living, etc.	**2. Resistance** Resist "what is" and stay in the relationship.	Kills the love in the relationship. Fighting, arguing, discontentment. Little chance of "happily-ever-after."
	3. Acceptance Accept "what is" and stay in the relationship.	Compatibility, contentment, potential for "happily-ever-after."
	4. Getting Out Remove yourself either from the relationship or the situation.	No relationship with current partner or change in the relationship.

A woman, Joan, sent me an email thanking me for writing *Intellectual Foreplay* because it "saved her twenty-year marriage." She was just on the verge of leaving her husband when she got a copy of the book. This formula provided her with a "looking glass" in which to observe her relationship, her responses, and the outcome that was being created. With it she realized that she was putting all her energy into *resisting* who her husband was and trying to change (control) him. Consequently, she felt powerless and unhappy. She chose instead to *accept* who he was, and from this new perspective, she was able to see her power in the relationship to make different choices and re-create the love in their relationship by focusing on her responses instead.

Your Response Options

If, after discussing the questions or spending time with your partner, you discover things that you are uncomfortable with or you feel they would have to change in order for you to be happy in the relationship, look to this chart and consider your options, the first of which is **negotiation**. You've undoubtedly heard, "Never go into a relationship thinking someone will change or that you can change them." However, there are instances of people changing their behavior and, depending on what it is you want changed, it's worth a try if you are explicit about what you are trying to do. Before you even attempt negotiation, however, it is wise to practice some self-observation and evaluate your motives. Are you asking your partner to change because the issue is really important, or are you just trying to establish control? Be honest with yourself. It may be that all that is necessary in order to restore happiness is for you to let go of the issue.

One of the particularly tricky things about negotiating for change is that at times this can hurt someone's feelings or cause them to get defensive. Often, when we think our concerns will hurt the feelings of one we love, we suppress the information, and it comes out in other ways—little barbs, teases, and hints (resistance)—that can hurt them even worse. A good policy to remember if you're going to give "constructive criticism" is to first ask yourself if it is purposeful. What is the purpose of telling them? Is it in support of their highest good and that of the relationship? Are you willing to stay with them to help them through their hurt to a more positive place?

How you approach negotiation also makes a great deal of difference to its success. Negotiation requires both partners to share how they feel and what they want and to look for solutions together. This means no passive-aggressive, nagging, or manipulative attempts, but rather honest, in-the-open negotiation for change. It could be as easy as simply saying, "I get upset when I climb in a bed that's damp and cold from the wet towel left on it all day. Could you please put the towel on the rack in the bathroom when you're done with it?" The problem and how it made you feel were presented, along with a possible solution. Your partner may not even realize that they are leaving the towel on the bed, and this simple request could raise their awareness and bring about change. There may also be more challenging situations where a mediator, such as a counselor or a therapist, would be helpful as a facilitator of communication between you and your partner.

Negotiation requires a certain willingness to communicate and to make change on the part of both partners, which may not always be present. Often the things we want our partners to address are deeply imbedded behaviors, lack of consideration, or major differences in values that aren't easily changed. There are things that your partner may not want to change, may not believe they can change, or may get defensive about. The whole scenario can leave you feeling powerless because, as mentioned earlier, we have no control or power over the event. This doesn't mean that negotiation is not an absolutely valid and potentially successful option, but be forewarned—people do not change easily. If you're going to attempt negotiation, be sure to be specific about the problem and how it affects you and offer alternatives or solutions. Remember, the idea here is to *solve* the problem, not complain about it. This is another arena in which knowing your own values and what is non-negotiable for you really helps, not only in choosing a partner, but also in knowing what you are and are not willing to change in yourself at a partner's request.

When we opt not to try negotiation or when it doesn't work, a common response is to **resist "what is."** Resistance takes place when we don't like something and yet choose to be in a relationship with our partner anyway. This choice (which we usually don't recognize as a choice) often results in nagging, barbed comments, sarcasm, ridicule, put-downs in front of others, arguing, and fighting, which all lead to basic unhappiness. When we resist what is, we find ourselves in a stalemate (or *with* a stale mate, or *being* one, if you'll pardon the pun).

People who engage in nagging, teasing, etc., often believe that what they are really doing is communicating and negotiating. Since they lack the skills to sit down and honestly communicate their needs and fears to their partners, they think that if they hint enough in the form of teasing, sarcasm, and put-downs, their partners will get the message and change. The reality, as all of us who have experienced it know, is that resentment, arguments, and great unhappiness are created instead. It is here where love dies in a partnership, self-esteem and self-worth are damaged, and relationships head downhill. Amazingly enough, this behavior often begins as a misguided, unskilled attempt at negotiation.

Michelle and Sam, one married couple whom we interviewed for *Intellectual Foreplay*, claimed that an important thing to know about your partner before getting seriously involved is how bright they like the lights in the bathroom. We must have looked perplexed, as they went on to explain that Sam likes them dim when he first wakes up and Michelle likes them bright for applying make-up. This became such a serious issue between them that it caused doubts about the viability of a lasting relationship. For those of us not in the middle of this battle, the light-bulb issue seems pretty unimportant. The problem, of course, wasn't really the "event" of the brightness of the lights but each of their responses to their partner (control/approval issues) and the outcome that they were creating.

Both Michelle and Sam entered into an ego-control battle, holding on tight to their perspective and resisting what the other person wanted. Negotiation wasn't an option because this basic preference wasn't going to change. What *was* negotiable, however, were solutions to the problem. When you are in a state of resistance, the situation begins to feel hopeless, as if there are no solutions. When you're not in the middle of the control battle, many options appear obvious. In this case, it might have meant installing a dimmer switch or a lighted make-up mirror or possibly even moving into a home with two bathrooms. When we are just trying to be heard (get approval) or change the other person (get control), we are not able to see the resources available to us.

The outcome can be satisfactory for both partners without either having to change their preferences if they are able to take a step back, regain perspective, let go of the ego-needs, and choose their responses. From there, they will be able to see many viable solutions, if they exist.

When your partner's answers match your own or match your expectations, or when negotiation is successful and the desired change takes place, it is easy to choose the third option, which is to **accept "what is."** We graciously accept the "event" when we like what we see and hear. Accepting what is, however, is not only reserved for times when we find it easy to do so. It is necessary to accept traits or habits about others even when it is not our first choice. Rather than negotiating change in the other person, acceptance requires a change in yourself; often it requires just an internal shift, or a reframing of the problem. For instance, your partner doesn't do dishes, you know he/she doesn't do dishes, and no amount of negotiating, arguing, or begging will get them to do dishes. Continued resistance isn't an option because it will kill the love in the relationship. In this case, dishes may not have a heavy enough weight to break up the relationship, so you simply accept that your partner doesn't do dishes. From this place of acceptance, you can consider some of the options: 1) you are the one who does the dishes or 2) you hire someone to do the dishes. You may even justify the outcome by recognizing a chore your partner does that you don't like.

When we take a moment to observe ourselves-and let go of our resistance—our control-and-approval dramas—we can more easily move into acceptance and thus stand a greater chance of creating happily-ever-after. *If you go into a relationship fully knowing the habits, traits, and morals of your partner, and if you choose to continue in the relationship anyway, you are in essence making the choice to accept those habits, traits, and morals.* There are some things, however, that we simply cannot accept as part of our lives. This is why it is so important to explore the relationship before getting too deeply involved. It is essential that you are aware of what you are choosing to accept. As you go through *Intellectual Foreplay,* remember to refer to your values and goals to help you determine what you will and will not accept.

If you encounter behaviors and beliefs that you do not want to accept into your life, it is still necessary to let go of resistance and accept who the other person is. However, from this resourceful state, you may choose to wish them well—and wish them out of your life—by choosing the fourth option: **getting out.** Getting out doesn't necessarily mean totally discontinuing the relationship. It may mean changing the relationship to a friendship or a business relationship rather than a romantic one, or it may mean getting out of a situation altogether. No matter what form of getting out you choose, it usually isn't an easy choice, even when we are absolutely positive that it is the right thing to do. Getting out tends to threaten our desire to love and to be loved, making us fear that we won't have love in our lives if we leave a relationship. Buying into this fear is dangerous and can trap us in unhealthy situations.

Years ago I was complaining (resisting what was) to a trusted friend, Adam, about a relationship I was in. After patiently listening, he stopped me and said, "Eve, I've been listening to you complain about the same things for a year now. I was just wondering if ten years from now you will still be complaining or if you are going to make some changes." He then asked, "Is there anything I can do to support you in taking the next step?" This comment hit me like a brick. What Adam didn't know was that I had been complaining for *another* full year prior to meeting him. Most of us have had the experience of staying in a relationship long after any signs of value are gone. Through our inaction, we create an unhealthy lifestyle for ourselves and for our partners. Getting out is seldom an easy thing to do; however, there are times when it is the best choice we can make for the good of all involved.

The Power of Choice

I mentioned "pure" choices earlier. A pure choice is one that obviously falls into one of the four options: negotiation, resistance, acceptance, or getting out. It is helpful to realize that there will be times when your choices are not clearly one option or another, but rather a creative mixture. For example, sometimes attempting to change a situation or your partner's behavior falls under "negotiation"; other times, it may be combined with the "getting out" option. For example, if you aren't successful at negotiating with a partner to reliably take your phone messages, rather than getting out of the relationship, you might opt to get out of the *situation* by getting your own voice-mail number.

Be aware that sometimes you may consciously choose one option while your emotions unconsciously choose another. For example, on an intellectual level you may choose to accept what is or to get out of a situation, but in actuality, your emotions are still holding onto some resistance. Mixed choices aren't problematic, unless resistance is part of the mixture. Resistance always contaminates our efforts to make healthy changes by bringing in control-and-approval issues.

When we suppress or stuff our emotions about a situation instead of truly accepting and transcending them, all we manage to do is delay the resentment and delay the problem (probably just long enough to get married, and then they resurface!). If you find that you are simply enduring and/or ignoring something that bothers you, you haven't truly managed to let go of the control-and-approval issues and are still resisting your partner or your choice. The result is continued discomfort with the situation while managing to cope anyway. True acceptance is more peaceful than enduring or ignoring the problem. If you find that you are suppressing your feelings or merely enduring a situation, return to a state of self-observation, return to your goals and values, and make a new choice about how you want to respond to the situation.

Ironically, acceptance is required in order to create any healthy outcome. Even if you negotiate successfully, you still must settle into a state of acceptance with the results. If you choose to get out of a relationship, you still must accept what is and let go of your ego-needs for control or approval or you will drag the same drama into your next relationship. Sometimes we decide to get out and then resist our own decision for a while. In order to be okay with any decision, we must combine it with acceptance.

One woman, Cindy, was feeling very unsure about a potential partner and was therefore unwilling to go forward in the relationship. She was, however, also unwilling to get out. Consequently, her potential partner was getting frustrated and getting to be less "potential" daily (is the root word of potential "potent?"). By default, Cindy was making a decision. Opportunities (events) can come and go. Every response leads to an outcome, which is then a new event to which we need to respond. Even "no choice" is a response that creates an outcome. As you explore the style of a potential partner through *Intellectual Foreplay,* observe yourself—your feelings, words, actions, tone of voice—and choose how to respond to your partner. Thus you will discover the power you have for creating healthy— or unhealthy—relationships.

Here is an example of the choices one can make when confronted with an event. In one family, the husband and father, Eric, is the one who always drives whenever the family goes anywhere. Being an intelligent man with a lot on his mind, he does not always pay full attention to his driving (or at least it seems that way to his passengers, which is as equally valid as the truth to them because it is their perceived experience of the event). Consequently, the family is always on the edge of their seats, stressed and afraid that they will get in an accident while their lives are in his hands. Remember, this is the event: Eric drives in a way with which the passengers are uncomfortable.

The passengers now have the four choices mentioned above. They can negotiate, resist, accept, or get out of the relationship or situation. Let's look at these options. They can **negotiate** with Eric to change the way he drives, which may work beautifully if he is willing and able to change. This option will require that they explain to him how they feel, what scares them specifically, and what they want. *Being specific is important when negotiating for a behavioral change.* If they just say, "We want you to drive better," this won't give him any information about what "better" means. This will be a particular problem if he doesn't feel he was driving poorly in the first place. Therefore, it may be better to say, "I would be more comfortable if you put on your brakes when you first see the brake lights on the cars ahead instead of waiting until we are really close, because it doesn't appear that you see them stopping and that scares me," or "I'm uncomfortable when you drive down the middle of two lanes, drift from lane to lane, and change lanes without looking over your shoulder."

Resistance is an option that is often taken by default, by taking no other course of action. If negotiation is unsuccessful or untried, and if the passengers don't take a moment to observe themselves, they will resist the way that Eric drives; they will continue driving with him and continue to be unhappy, scared, and resentful. It is in this area of choice where the people with the problem (the passengers) often feel totally powerless and completely miserable. They think that their gasps, slamming on imaginary brakes on the passenger side of the car, put-downs and back-seat driving are communication enough and that the driver ought to see that they are uncomfortable and change. The only way for change, as they see it, is for the other person to do the changing. They are waiting for something outside of themselves to make them feel better (i.e., they're waiting for a new and improved event). Often, this is where arguments, resentment, dirty looks, talking behind the other's back, complaining, and nagging show up. The choice to resist what is and stay in the situation always leads to stressful, unhealthy exchanges in a relationship.

Another option the passengers have is to **accept** that this is the way Eric drives, recognize he hasn't gotten into an accident yet, and continue driving with him without resentment or constant fear. This is often a hard one to understand, but the truth of the matter is that Eric doesn't think that his driving is a problem, and it is possible for the passengers to accept this belief also, therefore eliminating the problem. In other words, they change their response instead of changing the event.

If the passengers take a moment to self-observe, they will discover that the discomfort they are feeling is their need for control. When Eric is driving, they are out of control. When they argue and nag, they are in resistance rather than being resourceful. If they recognize this and take a few deep breaths to let go of this need and get centered, they will be *choosing a response* instead of just reacting. Since negotiation hasn't worked and resistance is not a healthy option, they can choose to accept what is (change themselves) and/or get out.

Of course, accepting that something is what it is doesn't necessarily mean that it is acceptable *in your life*. Sometimes, when you have accepted what is, the most reasonable next step is option number four: **getting out**. Now, in the case of the driving problem, this could, in severe cases, lead to a family break-up simply as a result of unhealthy communication and lack of problem-solving skills. It is however, somewhat unlikely that the partner or passengers would choose to leave the family relationship solely due to his driving. They could, however, choose not to be passengers with Eric anymore. They could get out of the car or negotiate to take on the task of driving. This would be a powerful choice.

Choices and outcomes are not isolated; they are not made in a vacuum. Every choice leads to a new outcome, which leads to a new need for a response, and on and on. Ultimately, life is merely a series of events and choices that lead to new events and choices. If the family no longer chooses to drive with Eric, he will react, which will lead to a need for a new response from the family. There are a multitude of variables. Hence, self-observation and a return to a centered, conscious state are imperative for making healthy choices.

Part of self-observation is looking to see if you play a part in the event. For instance, it is possible that Eric drives the way he does because he's in a hurry due to the family not being ready to leave on time. It's also possible that he's distracted by their conversations or their choice of music, etc. In this case, they would have to confront the possibility that they are partially responsible for the event. Though it is seldom a pleasant fact to face, if we look closely, we often find that we play a part in creating a situation. If we want a change, we must start with ourselves.

> On a separate piece of paper, practice exploring the power of your choices. Pick any situation that you have been in with a partner (or family member) and imagine the different ways that you could have responded. How do the outcomes change when you choose to negotiate, resist, accept, or get out?

As you go through *Intellectual Foreplay,* remember that your true power lies in your ability to choose responses in alignment with your goals and values. *It is in our response that our power lives. Empowerment comes from choice. Right choice comes from knowledge. Knowledge comes from asking. Wisdom comes in the listening. Change comes from taking action.*

Letting Go of Your Shiny Pennies

Through the ages, people have hunted raccoons by drilling a hole in a log and putting a shiny penny in the hole. A raccoon comes along, sees the shiny penny, and, being the curious type, tries to get the penny out. The problem for the coon is that when his paw is around the penny, he can't get his paw out of the hole in the log. When the hunters come along, all the raccoon has to do to free himself is let go of the penny. The raccoon, however, so engulfed in his need for the penny, never sees that his demise is simply due to his own lack of willingness to let go of the problem.

Whenever you're looking at problems in your relationships with your family or partner, first look within and see if it is simply a "shiny penny" you're holding onto or if change truly needs to take place. If it is just a shiny penny, with a little reframing or an internal shift, you can eliminate the problem. The wonderful thing about this place of acceptance, or letting go of the problem, is that often, once you've let go, a multitude of creative solutions will come into your awareness. Sometimes the person will automatically change their behavior once you stop letting it bother you and/or stop nagging them. When we are most stuck on something, we are least likely to discover solutions and options. Often, a solution is as simple as dropping the penny. Then we might find our answer on the other side of the coin.

A woman, Nancy, came to one of my parenting workshops and complained about the mess that was always in her son Jeff's room (the event). She explained that she was constantly telling him to clean it up, which he wouldn't do. Her response was to **resist**: to be upset, nag, and complain. The outcome, of course, was stressed family relationships, arguments, and general unhappiness. I asked her to take a moment to self-observe and determine whose problem this actually was. From a place of observation, she was able to see that the problem was hers, not her son's. She was experiencing a need to control, but Jeff was completely content with his room the way it was. Or, even more likely, he was completely content with resisting his mother's control.

In this situation negotiating wasn't working, resisting was killing their relationship, and getting out of the relationship wasn't an alternative. That left her with the option of accepting that Jeff's room was a mess and he didn't want to clean it. From a true place of acceptance, she could then make several choices. She could hire someone, but since Jeff was a teenager, he didn't want anyone in his room, and she didn't want to pay for it. She could continue forever attempting to get him to clean the room, which would likely lead to more control battles, or, among other options, she could stop caring that the room was a mess. She could decide that the room belonged to Jeff and, as long as his health wasn't jeopardized, allow him to keep his room any way he chose. When Nancy chose to accept and let go, harmony was restored. Ironically, shortly after Nancy dropped the control battle, she was surprised to find that Jeff suddenly cleaned his room.

John Bradshaw, author of *Bradshaw on The Family*, describes families (or relationships) as mobiles. Each member or partner is suspended in perfect balance with the others. If one person wants another to move (change), they must realize that they cannot reach that person from their own position. (In other words, they are powerless to change the other person.) However, if they simply shift their own position (accepting and becoming centered) and change their responses to the other person, the other person will change in relationship to them. Event + Response = Outcome.

The Choice Is Yours

We are responsible for our responses, which lead to our *internal* outcomes (happiness, peace of mind, resentment, etc.). However, when it comes to the *external* outcome or situation, or a relationship outcome, it is not only our responses that determine the equation. Our partners' responses are another essential factor. The formula for external outcomes tends to look more like this:

EVENT + MY RESPONSE + YOUR RESPONSE = OUTCOME

For instance, I may decide to "accept what is" and stay in the relationship, but my partner may decide to "get out." The combined responses create an outcome, which is a new event to which I must respond. We are in control of our internal outcomes (how we feel, behave, believe); however, the external event or situation, while we play a huge part in it, may not be totally up to us.

All of this brings to mind the truth of the Serenity Prayer and explains, in part, its usefulness. "Lord, grant me the serenity to accept the things I cannot change; the courage to change the things I can; and the wisdom to know the difference." In other words, we need to take a careful look at what we're getting into in order to make choices about what we want to attempt to change, what we want to accept into our lives, and what we want no part in. The rest we must leave in the hands of a Higher Power.

When you ask your partner questions and receive information, remember that the answers are merely the event, the "what is." You *always* have choices about how to respond, which leads to what is created for you. Empowerment comes from choice—our ability to respond. If you continue into a relationship knowing that there are certain trouble areas, you are not a victim. You are a responsible person who chose the set of circumstances that you will have to face. If you go into a relationship without asking, exploring, and researching, you still are not a victim. You are a person who did not take responsibility for checking into the circumstances that you chose and now must face. *Either way, through action or inaction, the choice is yours.*

Even the best questions and conscientious efforts, of course, can be answered with lies and concealed information. In part, this is out of your hands; however, there are some ways to avoid getting caught in this trap. Pay attention to the "yellow lights" or "red flags" that are triggered within you. Take the time to self-observe and get centered in your heart. *Listen to your intuition.* When we are centered in our hearts, we can use our heads. When we are in our heads alone, we miss a lot of information that our hearts and bodies tell us. Our bodies often give us signals before we are consciously aware of a problem. If you have a bad feeling about someone, *pay attention.* To a reasonable extent, listen to what others say and compare it with your experience. Do others' opinions or experiences of your potential partner match your own?

Be aware of whether the things your partner says match the things your partner does. If they tell you they're monogamous and you catch them with someone else, this action should speak louder than their words. Someone who *believes* in monogamy may not interest you as much as someone who *behaves* in a monogamous manner. If they tell you that good health is important to them but all they want to do is smoke, drink, eat, and watch television, take these actions as the real answer.

Here are a few questions you may want to continually ask yourself as you explore the questions in this book:

What is my response to that question (or to my partner's answer)?

In ten years, what will my response to that question or answer likely be?

Can I let go of that concern, or am I uncompromising on that?

How much does this matter to me?

How negotiable am I? How negotiable is my partner?

Do my partner and I communicate well?

Are we able to honestly share concerns?

Are the answers I'm hearing in alignment with the behavior I'm seeing?

Asking these questions in the back of your mind as you discuss other questions with your partner, and giving credence to your honest answers to yourself, will surely assist you in making the right choices.

The questions in *Intellectual Foreplay* will facilitate the discovery of many areas that are —or are not— in alignment with your values. Remember to return to Event + Response = Outcome. Once you've become aware of who your partner is (the event, or what is) and you've decided to stay in the relationship, *you have decided to accept* your partner the way they are and to accept their qualities, positive and negative, into your life (your response). Consequently, you have also accepted the outcome. Take responsibility for your decisions; use some foresight and really look at what you're getting into and what you are choosing. Once you've decided that you're willing to accept the "whole package" of your partner, the good and the not-so-desirable, then recognize you're responsible for your own happiness.

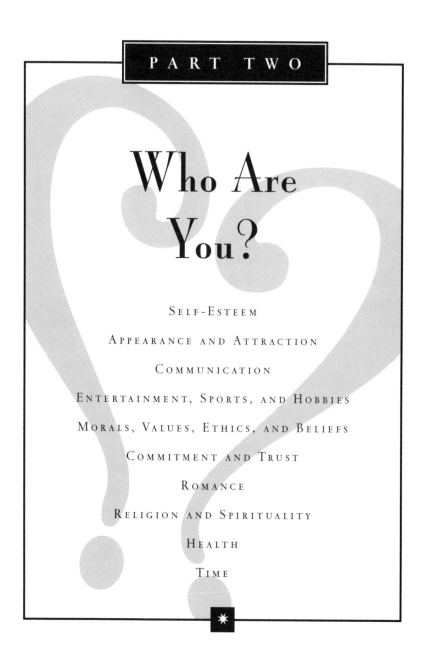

CHAPTER FOUR

Self-Esteem

elf-esteem is all-pervading. Every conversation and every interaction are affected by the self-esteem of each partner. Therefore, this category of questions is the first that needs to be addressed individually by each partner, but not necessarily the first category to be discussed together. The questions in this chapter can be intense and challenging to answer. If it makes you each more comfortable, take some time alone with these questions before you share your answers with a partner. Feel free to jump ahead to lighter, easier topics when you first begin *Intellectual Foreplay,* but be aware of those that you avoid, and make sure that you return to them.

If people don't love themselves or treat themselves with respect, you can bet that they don't know how to have a healthy relationship with someone else. The most important ingredient to "happily-ever-after" with someone else is to create the potential for happily-ever-after with yourself. If you find that your self-esteem is low, develop a positive relationship with yourself before trying to do the same with a partner. If you are already in a relationship, work on your self-esteem simultaneously.

Self-esteem has been the focus of a lot of misunderstanding. People often think of it as the same as ego or pride. I have heard people talk about how raising self-esteem is a selfish goal, a "me, me, me"-focused endeavor. Part of my personal mission is to raise people's awareness and create a more expansive definition of self-esteem. The California Legislature's Task Force to Promote Self-Esteem and Personal and Social Responsibility was made up of national self-esteem experts who together defined self-esteem as *"appreci-ating my own worth and importance and having the character to be accountable for myself and to act responsibly toward others."* This definition broadens the meaning of self-esteem to include its effect on others.

Think of the qualities of someone you consider to have high self-esteem. Words like confident, enthusiastic, responsible, clear, energetic, positive, funny, friendly, and kind, among others, likely come to mind. Wouldn't we all like to be around people with these qualities? A person's self-esteem affects everyone around them. If they have high self-esteem, the people around them are uplifted. If they have low self-esteem, the people around them feel as if their energy is being sucked out of them. When we have enhanced our self-esteem, we have more to offer those whom we encounter throughout the day. Our families, our co-workers, and our friends benefit. It makes perfect sense. If you start with tap water, whether you use it to make lemonade, tea, or coffee, the end result won't taste as good as if you had made it with fresh spring water. In much the same way, all your relationships are improved when a main ingredient—you—is refreshing from the start.

Consider the qualities of small children. They are playful, honest, fun-ny, spontaneous, in the moment, authentic to their feelings, curious, nat-ural learners, creative, imaginative, loving, risk-takers, adventurous, and on and on. These qualities are present not only in the children around us; they are also the qualities of the children we once were (the essence of the inner child). They didn't go away when we got older; they just got covered up. We still contain all the qualities of our inner children.

 List your good qualities. What do you like, admire, and appreciate about yourself? What are your strengths, skills, and talents?

Our self-esteem has been covered up with a layer of beliefs based on things that significant people said to us as we were growing up. Things such as, "You'll never amount to anything," "Don't be so stupid," or "I knew I couldn't count on you. I guess if I want something done, I'd better do it myself." Somewhere along the line, we took ownership of these statements, turning them into limiting beliefs about ourselves. The result is low self-esteem that limits our willingness to truly embrace life. Signs of this are comments or thoughts such as, "I can't," "I'm not worthy," or "I shouldn't even try." Fearing hurt, we become afraid to take risks, to love, or to stretch our perceived limits.

What limiting beliefs have you taken ownership of? These may be beliefs such as, "I can't sing," or "I am not qualified to share my opinions," or "If only I were smarter, maybe then people would love me," or "My brother was always my parents' favorite." They may even be relationship-limiting beliefs such as, "I am not lovable," or "I just can't make relationships work." How do they affect your willingness to participate fully in life? How do these beliefs affect your relationships?

Raising your self-esteem isn't a process of going out and finding something you've lost or never had; it is a matter of growing who you really are while letting go of who you really aren't. It is simply a matter of letting go of false beliefs that have distorted your view. Our challenge, indeed one of the main reasons we are here, is to uncover our true essence, let go of the ego-dramas that we have bought into, and shine our souls brightly in the world by living in alignment with the qualities with which we were born. Living in alignment with our esteemed self means that the choices we make in the world are actions that are respectable, that we feel good about. These are choices that are in alignment with our goals and values and that support the growth and benefit of others as well as ourselves. Doing the exercises in Chapter Two on values identification, and referring back to them periodically, will support your efforts to align your actions with your values.

Self-esteem isn't global. You may have high levels of esteem in the arena of work but feel insecure in your ability to maintain a relationship. You may be confident about your ability to communicate but have low self-esteem about your physical being. Self-esteem isn't something that you have or don't have. It is something you have *easy access* to in certain areas and *blocked access* to in other areas. Having high self-esteem doesn't mean that you never have self-doubt or low moments, but rather that when you do, you know they aren't permanent and you know how to recover from them. You know that who you really are isn't your weak, fearful self, but rather your strong, centered, capable self.

As you consider choosing a partner, know that their level of self-esteem will surely impact the relationship. If someone doesn't feel deserving of love, they often find ways to sabotage the relationship so that their outer reality matches their inner belief system. If your partner has healthy self-esteem, they will be more willing to take the risk of sharing their thoughts and feelings and to take actions that support the well-being of the relationship. If they have self-esteem, they will be less likely to play games or get overly jealous or possessive. If they have a strong sense of themselves, they will be better able to support you emotionally, intellectually, physically, and spiritually.

You'll note, as you go through this chapter, that questions related to emotions have been included here. Although emotions and self-esteem are not the same thing, they relate closely to each other. When we are esteemed, we recognize that although we *have* emotions, we are not our emotions. Emotions and how we handle them are very important: they either contribute to our celebration of life or signal that something is amiss and needs our attention. How we handle them, express them, and, sometimes, cope with them is directly related to our deeper knowledge of who we really are.

Remember, you are not asking these questions to find out what is wrong with yourself or your partner, but rather to get to *know* yourself and your partner. The questions in this chapter are not designed to lower your self-esteem by spotlighting problems, but rather to raise your awareness. The good news is that, if you're not comfortable with your responses (i.e., with yourself), you have the ability to change! Levels of self-esteem are not fixed. With some concentrated effort, you can raise your self-esteem to a healthy, productive state, but everyone must do it for themselves. You cannot "fix" your partner if they have low self-esteem—they have to do it. Conversely, if you have low self-esteem, no partner, regardless of how wonderful, will fill the void that Self-love must fill. (Self, here, is defined as your soul, your divine nature.)

The first steps toward raising your esteem are Self-remembrance, Self-observation, and alignment. Remember who you really are, observe yourself, and realign with that essence.

QUESTIONS TO ASK EACH PARTNER

❖ Describe yourself.

❖ Do you like yourself the way you are, or would you have to change to be happy with yourself? Explain.

❖ What, specifically, do you like or dislike about yourself?

❖ What do you respect about yourself?

❖ Do you feel respected by others? What qualities do others respect in you?

❖ What have your major life successes been?

❖ What are your main strengths, skills, and talents?

❖ How do your strengths serve your relationships?

❖ When are you happiest?

❖ What makes you sad?

❖ In which ways are you satisfied with the way you are living your life?

❖ In which areas of your life do you feel secure about yourself?

❖ In which areas of your life do you feel vulnerable or insecure about yourself?

❖ Do you tend to approach new situations with confidence or fear?

❖ How do you handle fear?

❖ How does fear affect your accomplishments?

❖ Do you have any phobias? If so, how do your phobias impact your life?

❖ In which areas of your life do you see yourself as independent?

❖ In which areas of your life are you dependent, and on whom?
  Is anyone dependent on you? For what?

❖ Are you comfortable spending time alone, or do you need
  people around you?

❖ Do you need to be in a relationship to be happy or feel whole?
  How do you feel about yourself when you're single?

❖ Are you comfortable being loved? Are you able to receive love,
  and do you feel that you are worthy of it?

❖ Are you comfortable allowing yourself to fully love someone?

❖ Have you ever experienced "unconditional love"?
  What does this term mean to you?

❖ What do you consider to be your responsibilities in life?

❖ Are you generally pessimistic or optimistic?

❖ Who or what controls your life?

❖ Do you ever feel like a victim in life? Under what circumstances?

❖ In which ways are you the creator of what happens to you?

❖ In which ways do you take risks?

❖ How often do you feel depressed, and what tends to put you into a depression? How do you get out of depression?

❖ How do you feel about saying "No" to others?

❖ How do you want to be supported when your self-esteem is low?

❖ Do situations at work affect your self-esteem? If so, how do you handle that? How do you cope?

❖ How do you handle receiving criticism?

❖ How do you give criticism?

❖ What do you tend to put yourself down about?

❖ Have you ever received repeated comments or criticism from different people on the same personality trait or behavior? If so, what was it, and how did you handle the comments?

❖ How much weight do you give to other people's opinions of you? Of your partner? Do you listen or get defensive?

❖ How do you feel about receiving compliments? How do you feel about giving compliments?

❖ Do you need a lot of verbal reinforcement from your partner to feel good about yourself?

❖ In which ways do you tend to build or destroy the self-esteem of others?

❖ How do you feel about your age?

❖ How comfortable are you with your race?

❖ In which areas of your life do you have strong willpower?

❖ In which ways are you self-disciplined?

❖ In which areas of your life is your willpower weak?

❖ Under which circumstances do you trust your intuition?

❖ Under which circumstances do you see yourself as competitive?

❖ Under which circumstances do you see yourself as cooperative? A team worker?

❖ In which situations do you see yourself as a follower or a leader?

❖ Are you affectionate? Are there situations in which you are more or less comfortable being affectionate?

❖ Do you like hugs? Are there any situations in which you don't like hugs?

❖ Do you feel comfortable/safe expressing your emotions within your relationship? Are there any emotions that you avoid feeling or talking about?

❖ Are you able to cry? Under what circumstances? How often?

❖ How do changes in diet/sleep/stress affect your moods?

❖ When you are in a bad mood, how do you want your partner to treat you?

❖ How do you react when your partner displays emotional stress (do you tend to get angry, impatient, frustrated, or withdraw; do you offer comfort, support, etc.)?

❖ What makes you particularly angry (problems at work, traffic, etc.)?

❖ How do you handle anger?

❖ Do you feel comfortable with your ability to control your temper?

❖ Have you ever hurt a partner physically when you were angry?

❖ Do you hit or throw things when you are angry?

❖ Is there anyone in your life for whom you feel hatred? If so, how do you handle such a strong emotion, and how does it affect your life?

❖ What are your signs of stress?

❖ How do you handle stress?

❖ How do you treat others when you are stressed?

❖ Do you take action when you need a change, or do you complain while waiting for change?

❖ How do you feel about your ability to make decisions?

❖ In which situations do you see yourself as having a problem-solving attitude?

❖ How do you feel about seeking counseling for emotional problems?

❖ How do you express yourself and your personality—e.g., with words, visually (with clothes, hair, jewelry, etc.), or through art, dance, song, poetry?

❖ Have you ever considered suicide? Under what circumstances? What stopped you?

❖ Are you interested in, committed to, or tolerant of personal growth or self-improvement? For yourself? For your partner?

❖ In which ways do you seek out personal growth?

❖ Do you believe in the "inner child?" If so, in what ways are you able to please your child-self?

❖ In which situations are you able to be childlike, playful, or silly?

❖ Are you able to take care of yourself (financially, physically, emotionally, etc.)?

❖ Do people come to you for advice? Who and on what topics?

❖ On which topics do you feel competent giving advice?

❖ What do you see as your personal effect on the world? How do you contribute to society?

OBSERVATIONS OF YOUR PARTNER

❖ What qualities do you respect in your partner?

❖ What do you see as your partner's strengths, skills, and talents?

❖ Do you see your partner as independent or dependent?

❖ Does your partner tend to criticize you, put you down, or build you up? Which do you do to your partner?

❖ Does your partner tend to put himself/herself down?

❖ Does your partner brag in an offensive way (showing false self-esteem or need for approval), or are they able to share their good qualities in a pleasant way (healthy self-esteem)? *[A clue to this answer is in self-evaluation: do you feel closer to them after they have shared their successes (self-esteem), or do you feel pushed away or put down (ego)? Ego and conceit are not the same as true self-esteem.]*

❖ How well does your partner receive compliments?

❖ How does your partner treat you when they are under stress?

❖ Is your partner capable of a full range of emotions? Are they playful? Silly? Serious? Can they laugh and cry?

❖ How does your partner react if you cry?

❖ How does your partner treat you when you feel emotional?

❖ How can you tell if your partner wants time alone or is depressed? How do they handle it, and how do you respond?

SELF-OBSERVATIONS:

❖ How does your partner contribute to your self-esteem?
  Do you tend to allow your partner to lower or raise your self-esteem?

❖ How do you contribute to your partner's self-esteem?

❖ Do you feel respected by your partner?

❖ Do you feel superior to, inferior to, or equal to your partner?
  In which ways?

❖ Do you like your partner just the way they are, or would they have to change for you to be happy with them? Explain.

❖ Do you feel safe when your partner is angry?

❖ How do you support your partner when their self-esteem is low?

❖ How do you support each other in taking risks or in stepping beyond perceived limits?

✳

CHAPTER FIVE

Appearance and Attraction

e have a single friend, Jake, in his twenties, who judges all his potential dates by whether he considers them to be "book worthy"—meaning whether he would take the time to go through *Intellectual Foreplay* with them. One day we were out to breakfast when a particularly shapely woman walked by. Jake looked her up and down, turned to me, and said, "Definitely book worthy!" I quickly reminded him that there is a *big* difference between "magazine worthy" and "book worthy"!

Appearance is one of the very first things we notice about a potential partner, and it is a very powerful component of attraction. It is likely that everyone, at one time or another, has gotten involved with someone simply because of physical attraction. In fact, it is because of this phenomenon that this book was created. Most of us need no help determining who and what is attractive to us; what we need help with is looking beyond attraction to the other necessities of a lasting relationship. Once all the other essentials are in place, attraction becomes the glue in a partnership. It's the added dimension that separates friendships from relationships.

Attraction and appearance aren't the same thing, however. Although you may appreciate how another person looks, you may not be attracted to them. At the same time, there are people who have "sex appeal" but who aren't considered pretty or handsome by most standards. Attraction is an element that is a bit of a mystery. It is one of those things that is hard to define and is different for everyone. If this point wasn't driven home in the last chapter, let me reiterate that self-esteem is a very attractive element in another person. Feeling good about yourself and feeling that you are a good option as a partner will facilitate others feeling good about you, too. *Who* we are and *how* we are also affect how others see us physically. I once knew a woman who, when we first met, looked relatively plain. As we got to know each other and became friends, I thought she was beautiful. After she stole money from me and lied to me, I thought she was ugly. The concept that "beauty is only skin deep" is true. Inner beauty has a definite effect on outer beauty.

Since appearance and attraction are often areas of great concern, it is useful to know how your partner feels about these topics. This doesn't mean that you need to change to accommodate their desires or compromise your own preferences. Just take everything as information, see how you both feel, and discover whether you are compatible. If you find that you are compromising your values by changing things that matter to you just to please your partner, take that as a sign of a need to work on your self-esteem. You do not need to compromise what is important to you to have the relationship you truly want.

Again, these topics—and thus this chapter—probably won't be discussed in the early stages of dating, but they certainly will affect the relationship from the start. Begin by reading through the questions and answering them yourself and observing your partner. Then, as things progress and it seems appropriate, broach the subject with your partner.

Questions to Ask Each Partner

❖ Do you feel attractive? What do you like about the way you look?

❖ Which personal characteristics do you find attractive, in yourself and in others?

❖ Which do you find more attractive, physical beauty or a good personality?

❖ Is physical beauty essential to your happiness (in yourself and in your partner)?

❖ Do you worry about aging or looking "youthful"?

❖ Do you worry about how your partner's looks will change over time?

❖ Do you have a preference for loose or tight clothing?
Sexy or conservative (on yourself and on your partner)?

❖ Do you consider dressing an art or a necessity?

❖ How important are fashions to you? Is style important?
Are coordinated colors important?

❖ How do you feel about you and your partner wearing matching clothes?

❖ What kinds of clothes do you like your partner to wear?

❖ Is there anything you don't want your partner to wear?

❖ If you didn't like something your partner was wearing
or their hairstyle, would you tell them?

❖ If your partner didn't like what you were wearing or your hairstyle,
would you want them to tell you?

❖ Are you willing to adjust your style to match your partner's preferences?

❖ How do you feel about lipstick or make-up (on yourself or on your partner)?

❖ How do you feel about long fingernails (on yourself or on your partner)? Nail polish?

❖ How much time do you spend each day on making yourself more attractive or on getting ready to go out?

❖ What is your opinion about shaving/not shaving (e.g., face, legs, armpits, pubic hair, etc.)?

❖ What are your preferences around hairstyles?

❖ Is it okay for your partner to make major changes in hairstyle, hair length, or shaving or not shaving without consulting you?

❖ If your partner asked you to shave, not to shave, or to change your hairstyle, would you do it?

❖ How would you handle a major weight gain (or loss) in your partner?

❖ Do you wear perfume/cologne?

❖ How do you feel about your partner wearing perfume/cologne?

❖ How would you handle it if your partner became disfigured?

❖ To what lengths would you go to feel attractive (operations, face lifts, steroids, plastic surgery, breast implants, liposuction, orthodontia, hair perms and coloring, hair implants, fasting, exercising, dieting, etc.)?

❖ What do you think about these procedures?

❖ To what extent have you already undergone these procedures?

❖ To what lengths would you go, at your partner's request, to be attractive to them? Would you undergo any of the procedures listed above?

❖ How do you feel about tattoos?

❖ Would you get a tattoo if your partner asked you to?

❖ How do you feel about pierced ears (on men and women)? Multiple ear piercings?

❖ How do you feel about body piercing—belly buttons, tongues, noses, etc.?

❖ Do you like to wear jewelry? How much? [A consideration in regard to wedding rings, excessive jewelry, costume jewelry, etc.] How do you feel about your partner wearing jewelry? How much?

OBSERVATIONS OF YOUR PARTNER

❖ What, specifically, attracts you to your partner?

❖ Do you like the way your partner looks?
What, specifically, do you like or dislike?

❖ Do you like the way your partner dresses?
What, specifically, do you like or dislike?

❖ Does your partner have any body odors you find offensive?
If so, are you willing to talk to them about it?

SELF-OBSERVATIONS

❖ How physically attracted are you to your partner?
Do you see the attraction enduring over time?

❖ Do you feel confident about your attractiveness?

❖ Do you feel confident about your partner's attraction to you?

❖ Are you comfortable with your weight and height? Your partner's?
Is this an area of sensitivity?

❖ If you could no longer visually see your partner,
would you still love them?

CHAPTER SIX

Communication

ne couple in a long-distance relationship, Kara and Vince, shared that they talked on the phone for hours and hours about the many topics in *Intellectual Foreplay.* Kara confessed that she became "addicted" to that level of intimate discussion. When she moved in with Vince and they were face to face all day, their conversations were reduced to day-to-day dialogue. She had fallen in love with him through their conversations and found it difficult when their time wasn't spent in deep communication. Vince felt that that level of conversation wasn't necessary when they had just spent the whole day together. After fighting her urge to go to the corner store to call him from a pay phone, they discussed the situation and found a compromise that worked for both of them. She let go of her need for that level of communication *all the time,* and he made it a point to pay more undivided attention to her each day.

A survey once asked a group of single people what the biggest complaint was in their life. The majority said, "Loneliness." The surveyors then asked a group of married people what their biggest area of concern was, and they too replied, "Loneliness." Even when we are in the full-time presence of another we can still experience loneliness—unless there is connection and communication. Communication is more than the simple exchange of information, however. Both people must clearly express their point (feelings, thoughts, information), and, at the same time, what they express needs to be heard and understood. Both skills—speaking with clarity and listening with focus—are simultaneously involved for both parties. *Webster's* defines communication as "to bestow or confer for joint possession." This is a wonderful image. When you give a gift to someone, you no longer possess it, because a thing is held by only one person at a time. However, with clear communication, when thoughts or ideas are shared, both people possess what is expressed. With poor communication, the person sharing walks away feeling that what they offered was never accepted; they are still the sole owners, so to speak, or at best, only part of what they offered was accepted. At the same time, the receiver may feel that the information wasn't given to them in a form they could get a grip on.

Clarity is a key concept in communication. In order for another to receive your message, you must state it clearly, being sure that you use the correct words and intonations and that you don't send mixed messages. Interestingly, when we string together the correct letters to form a word that carries a certain impact in the world, we call it "spelling." When someone wants to create a magical impact in the world, they string certain letters or symbols together to create a "spell." Our words are very powerful. They are felt for many years after the moment of utterance. When words are strung together, we call the result a "sentence." Our words can literally "sentence" someone to a life of feeling pain or pleasure. When you communicate with your partner, be careful that what you say is the "spell" that you mean to cast.

Intimacy (Into-Me-See) of communication is also a critical element, because without it, it is possible for two people who talk to each other regularly to still feel lonely or disconnected. Many of us were raised on superficial conversation, the surface information of daily life. Intimate communication serves to break through the surface to access deeper feelings, thoughts, and beliefs. True intimacy goes deeper than words and topics. It is the sense that you—your thoughts and feelings—are truly received and accepted. A give-and-receive of energy is experienced, even in the absence of words. This requires safety and vulnerability. When there is deep trust between people, it is safe to take risks—exploring thoughts, trying out new beliefs, sharing hurts and fears, and even experiencing and enduring conflict together.

Expressing our needs is a risk in itself; it makes us vulnerable. One of the main reasons we don't get our needs met is that we don't communicate them—we often don't feel safe taking that risk. When we feel that we are received through a filter of judgment, or when we encounter a lack of confidentiality, sharing becomes dangerous. If an intimate relationship is what you desire, examine your and your partner's sense of safety and vulnerability in your abilities to communicate.

Nonverbal communication is also very informative. A person's attitudes about life and toward other people are communicated not only in their words, but also in their tone of voice and body language. Be aware of (or wary of) one who always complains or carries a "victim" attitude. If you want someone who is positive about life, look for the evidence in their style of communication. Some people, even when saying nice things or agreeing with you, sound as if they are criticizing. There are others who say everything so sweetly that it becomes hard to believe in the sincerity of their words. This can be very damaging to one's sense of safety. Exaggeration and teasing can be among the most harmful barriers to intimacy and communication.

One of my friends was raised in a family that did a lot of bantering back and forth, teasing and using sarcasm as a means of communication. Because that was her family's style, she has no problem with being in a relationship in which she and her husband jokingly put each other down. I was raised in a family, however, in which put-downs were not allowed. The environment was one of "If you can't say something nice, don't say anything at all." Hence, it would not be comfortable for me to be in a relationship with a partner whose style incorporated teasing. It is important to be aware of and respectful of each other's styles and comfort zones in your daily communication.

Another couple, Jody and Sam, communicate by ordering each other around and constantly sound as if they are in a little fight. When I mentioned it to them, they both looked genuinely surprised, denying that there was any problem between them. They were both completely comfortable with their style of communicating, and any problem with it was my own.

Although it is important to be comfortable with each other's communication styles, it is also valuable to self-observe to be sure that you haven't fallen into a pattern of expressing yourself that you haven't really chosen. It may be that your natural style, derived from the way you were raised, isn't what you would choose if you approached a conversation consciously. Remember, too, that if you have children, they are going to learn their style of communication from you—and your partner.

Our values are communicated not only by what we say but by how well our words and our actions align. If we say one thing and do another, we transmit mixed communication. If we say no when we mean yes, or if we go ahead and do it anyway, we teach people not to listen to us when we say no. If we say that honesty is important to us but then ask our partner or child to tell someone on the phone that we aren't home when we are, we show them that honesty isn't really that important or that we consider its importance to be selective.

Trust and honesty are communication essentials. I once dated a man who found it easier to lie to people than to tell the truth, even when there was no apparent benefit to the lie. If we were at a party and wanted to leave, instead of saying to the host, "Thank you, we need to go. We're both tired," he would make up a lie about how we had another appointment to go to, even though it was ten o'clock at night. Watch out for people whose natural styles incorporate lying, because you can be sure that eventually lies will be told to you, too.

In addition to depth and style, there are also practical aspects of communication that are important. One couple, Diane and Tony, is faced with turmoil every time Tony neglects to give Diane her phone messages. She has responded to this challenge by filling their home with memo pads, which help, but he still forgets to let her know when someone has called for her or about upcoming parties they have been invited to. On the other side, Tony feels that Diane is on the phone too much. Perhaps forgetting to tell her who called is unconsciously a way to keep her off the phone. Problems like these are symptomatic of basic consideration issues that can affect a relationship even more deeply than whether or not a message is relayed.

One woman, Liz, has been dating Danny for over a year and has yet to discover a pattern to their communication in terms of frequency. While her preference is to check in every day by phone, he seems to be content with talking once a week or so. While he appears to be committed to the relationship, his own life is so busy that he just doesn't see the point of communicating more regularly. This discrepancy could be indicative of an underlying difference that, if not discussed and resolved, could damage the relationship. If they can look at this without getting caught in resistance and can accept each other's needs and look at the options that are available, they will be able to find a solution that satisfies them both.

What people choose to talk *about* can also affect a relationship. A person's sense of humor can communicate a lot about how they see the world. Jokes that are based in prejudice or ridicule can often be offensive. Some people spend all their time talking about the same topics, perhaps boring their partners to death. Others are content to talk forever about themselves but show no interest in hearing about their partners' feelings or interests. A few moments of self-observation to see how your own communication style—your listening skills and choice of subject matter—affects your relationships could be worth their weight in gold.

Technology has added an interesting twist to the world of communication. When answering machines first came out, people expressed resentment at reaching machines instead of the people they were calling. Now, when we call someone who doesn't have a machine, we think they are living in the Dark Ages. The same phenomenon is happening with email, the Internet, cell phones, and pagers. Although immediate accessibility can be quite convenient when you are trying to find your partner, it can be quite annoying when you can never get away from others on a date! One woman complained to me about how her boyfriend even answered the phone in the middle of making love! Pay attention to how you and your partner prioritize and guard your private time.

Some people who have been noncommunicative verbally, however, have found that the Internet and email have opened up a whole new realm for them to meet people, "date," and have conversations in the safety of their own homes. A man I worked with seldom spoke to any of his co-workers until he got email capabilities. Suddenly, he became quite expressive, writing regular emails to the whole staff.

A student in one of my relationship classes, Frank, took *Intellectual Foreplay* to the computer and used the questions with the people he met online. He and Linda used this as a means of connecting and determined that there was a definite foundation on which to build a relationship. They took the next step of meeting each other and continued their exploration in person. They are now happily engaged and living together, thankful that this useful tool guided them along the way.

Nowadays, computers bridge the categories of business, communication, time use, entertainment, and even sex and are becoming more and more of an issue in relationships. Just as Kara got "addicted" to telephone conversations with Vince, one can also get "addicted" to email conversations. While this does open new possibilities for finding a mate, you have to be careful, because it is far easier to lie in a chat room or an email than it is in person or over the phone. Also, a false sense of intimacy can be created when you are carrying on long conversations with someone you have never met. Be careful about revealing intimate details of your life to someone you don't know, and be watchful as to whether a partner is able to communicate with you directly as well as through electronic means.

You'll find that this chapter has more observation questions than questions to ask each other. Good communication is a perceived experience. It is possible to talk *at* someone without talking *with* someone, and it is possible to hear your partner's words without receiving their message. Ironically, good communication shows up more in what you *do* than in what you *say* you do. While you may not choose to talk about these questions at the beginning of a relationship, be sure to observe how you relate to each other from the very start! Feel free to share your observations and perceptions with each other for additional clarification as your relationship progresses.

Questions to Ask Each Partner

❖ In which situations do you consider yourself to be a
good communicator?

❖ In which situations would you like to improve your
communication skills?

❖ Do you consider yourself to be a good listener?

❖ Do you tend to interrupt or finish other people's sentences?

❖ How often would you like to talk with someone you are dating?
Does your preference change as a relationship develops?

❖ Are you able or willing to listen and talk when you are doing
other things?

❖ How often do you feel it is necessary to discuss important topics
and relationship issues?

❖ Are there any topics that you don't feel comfortable talking about
with your partner? If so, which ones? Do you know why?

❖ Are there topics you love to explore in conversation?

❖ How do you feel about teasing and sarcasm?

❖ How comfortable are you with disagreement? Do you like to debate?

❖ Are you good at keeping in touch with friends?

❖ How accessible are you? Do you carry a pager? Do you carry a cell
phone? What are your feelings about them?

❖ Do you have email? How often do you check it?

❖ How do you prefer to stay in touch with others: letters, email, or the phone?

❖ Are you good about returning phone calls and answering mail?

❖ Do you consider your mail and email private? How do you feel about your partner wanting to read it?

❖ What kinds of jokes do you consider funny? Do you like to tell jokes?

❖ Do you cuss or use foul language? Does it bother you when others do?

❖ How do you feel about silence in a conversation? Does it make you uncomfortable; do you try to fill it?

QUESTIONS TO EXPLORE AS A COUPLE

❖ Do you and your partner have language barriers—do you both speak the same language and are you both at the same level of understanding? Is one or both of you hearing impaired (in which case, how do you communicate)? If such barriers exist, how do they affect the depth of your communication?

❖ Do you feel you and your partner communicate well—in both listening and understanding each other?

❖ Are you and your partner able to express what you want?

❖ Do you and your partner talk about your feelings?

❖ Do you feel as though your communication together is sometimes intimate, or is it always superficial? Are you comfortable with the depth of your communication?

❖ Do you and your partner communicate with sincerity—or does your communication tend toward syrupy words, exaggerations, little white lies, etc.?

❖ Do you both get equal time to speak and be heard, or does one dominate the conversations?

❖ When you communicate with each other, what kind of style do you both tend to adopt? How does it affect you? (Are bickering, teasing, sarcasm, complaints, blame, or put-downs a recurring theme?) Are you comfortable with your mutual style of communication?

❖ Do you look each other in the eyes when you talk? Are you comfortable with looking each other in the eyes?

❖ Are you and your partner considerate of each other in terms of communicating upcoming events and parties, passing on messages, etc.?

OBSERVATIONS OF YOUR PARTNER

❖ Is your partner communicative? Is your partner a good listener?

❖ Is your partner's sense of humor in alignment with your own?

❖ Does your partner respond when spoken to? Do you feel acknowledged when you speak?

❖ Is your partner able or willing to listen and talk when they're doing other things?

❖ Does your partner tend to communicate in a positive or negative way? Do they generate solutions or merely complain about problems?

❖ Does your partner's tone of voice and body language match their message? (For example, do they say nice things in a biting tone of voice or make stabbing comments sweetly? Do they smile when they tell you something sad?)

❖ Does your partner use baby talk or switch into other tones of voice (nagging, little boy/girl, bossy, whiny, sarcastic, angry, impatient, sugary, etc.) that challenge your ability to listen?

❖ Does your partner's accent, use of slang, improper use of language, tone of voice, etc., bother you or get in the way when they're speaking with others?

❖ Does your partner cuss? Is their language offensive to you? To others?

❖ Does your partner interrupt you or finish your sentences?

❖ Does your partner complete their own sentences and thoughts when they speak?

❖ Does your partner tease you or make you the butt of humor? If so, does it happen in private? In public? Does it bother you?

❖ Does your partner discuss a variety and range of subjects, or are they virtually one-tracked?

❖ Does your partner appear interested in you and your answers to these questions, or only in answering them about him/herself?

❖ Does your partner only want to ask you the questions without answering them him/herself?

Self-Observations

❖ Are you satisfied with the way in which you and your
   partner communicate?

❖ Do you tend to communicate through arguing and bickering?

❖ Do you tend to communicate in a positive way or a negative way?
   (Is the glass half empty or half full?) Do you communicate problems
   or solutions?

❖ Do you feel safe sharing your feelings with your partner?
   Are there any topics that don't feel safe?

❖ When something bothers you, do you tend to just bring it up,
   or do you spend several days (or hours) trying to figure out how
   to approach the subject?

❖ Do you tend to want to talk things out and solve them before
   you go to sleep, or do you like to "sleep on it"?

❖ Are you generally interested in what your partner has to say,
   or do you find yourself "tuning them out"?

❖ How tolerant are you of your partner talking on the phone? Are you
   comfortable with their availability (to you *and* to others) via cell phone,
   email, pager, etc.?

✳

CHAPTER SEVEN

Entertainment, Sports, and Hobbies

y husband, Steven, is a boat captain and goes out on the ocean every day. I, on the other hand, work indoors in an office. When I come home from work, I want to get outside, get some sun and some exercise. Steven, however, has been in the sun exercising all day already and wants to relax inside. These differences can put a relationship to the test if you aren't comfortable doing things by yourself or with someone other than your partner—which, fortunately, I am.

How you like to spend your spare time, together or alone, can have a great impact on your relationship. Not only is this topic important in terms of what you do together, but it's also important in terms of your respect for each other. Life is made up of nothing but time. How you use that time is how you spend your life. Recreation is only one aspect of a relationship, yet it is an important one. If you look closely at the word "recreation," it is "re-creation," meaning "to create again." When you share your hobbies and interests or at least respect each other's, the relationship is repeatedly rejuvenated. When there are major incompatibilities, relationships tend to break down.

A married couple we know faces a challenge in this arena. Bonnie grew up in the United States, and her family often went to the movies as a form of entertainment. Her husband, Jeff, grew up in another country where going to the movies wasn't a popular thing to do. Now they always have to compromise. She doesn't go to the movies anywhere near as often as she'd like, and he goes far more often than he'd prefer.

You may encounter many stereotypic differences between men and women that can lead to challenges in the area of entertainment. She likes love stories, he likes action films. He wants to watch wrestling, she wants a soap opera. She wants to talk, he wants solitude. Jenny, a woman in her early fifties who went through *Intellectual Foreplay,* wrote to tell me about how she loved her husband dearly but couldn't stand how "involved" in sports he got. She shared that not only did he spend many hours in front of the television watching them, but he would scream, yell, and even swear after each play. Jenny was particularly upset that her husband would be in a bad mood for hours if "his" team didn't win.

It helps to know about these behaviors and preferences before you get into a serious relationship, but if you discover them after you are already involved, remember that these are the "events." Simply resisting your partner's ways will surely kill the love between you. Go back to the chart on E + R = O in Chapter Three and, after some self-observation, accept how your partner is and determine which response is most aligned with your values and goals.

The questions in this chapter will likely be one of the most comfortable to discuss with a partner, as the topic isn't as laden with deep values. Enjoy the process as a lighter means of getting to know each other and introducing each other to new forms of entertainment.

QUESTIONS TO ASK EACH PARTNER

❖ What do you like to do for entertainment?

❖ What are your favorite activities or hobbies, and how much time do you spend on them each week?

❖ How important is it to you that your partner participate in your favorite activities with you? Are you willing to share your sports, hobbies, or activities with your partner?

❖ What are your favorite:

movies?

books?

songs?

bands or musical groups?

sounds?

sights?

smells?

tastes?

❖ Which clubs or organizations do you belong to? How much time do these activities involve?

❖ Do you frequent a particular bar or place of entertainment? Where? How often?

❖ What kinds of movies do you like? How often do you like to go?

❖ Where do you like to sit in a theater?

❖ How many hours of television do you watch a day? How important is television to you?

❖ How do you feel about television in the bedroom?

❖ Do you think the number of hours of television per day should be limited for a healthy household or relationship?

❖ Are you available to other people while you're watching television? Is it a shared activity or an independent one?

❖ Who gets control of the remote control? Are you a channel changer? Do you ask the other person before you change the stations?

❖ What kind of shows do you like to watch on television? Are there television shows or types of shows that you "have" to watch? If so, which ones? Do you schedule your day around them?

❖ What sports or activities do you participate in?

❖ Are there any sports or activities that you "live for"? If so, which ones?

❖ How do you feel about extreme sports? Do you participate in them? If so, do you expect your partner to participate in them with you? What if they do not?

❖ Do you watch sports on television? How often? How much time do you spend watching them?

❖ Do you go to sporting events? How often? Which ones?

❖ How personally involved do you get with "your" team's performance? If they lose, does it make you angry or put you in a bad mood?

❖ How do you feel about amusement parks and fairs? Do you go on the "scary" rides? If so, do you expect your partner to go with you? How would you handle it if they didn't want to go?

❖ How much time do you spend on the computer and on the Internet?

❖ Do you go into chat rooms? Whom do you talk with, and how much time do you spend there?

❖ How do you like to spend weekend nights? Weeknights?

❖ How late do you like to stay out?

❖ Do you like to go to parties? How often? In general, how long do you like to stay (until the party's over, until after you've paid your social dues)?

❖ What kinds of music do you like?

❖ Do you go to concerts? What kind? How often?

❖ Do you like to dance? Any particular style? How often?

❖ Do you like to sing? In the shower? In the car? Around the house? Karaoke?

❖ Do you like to go to plays, musicals, operas, or orchestra performances?

❖ How much time do you spend reading in a week? Is this ever a shared experience (reading to each other or talking about the material), or is it always independent?

❖ Do you think you read too much or too little? How does reading affect your relationship?

❖ What do you collect?

❖ In what ways are you artistic?

❖ What kind of art do you like?

❖ Do you like museums? What kind? How often do you like to go?

❖ Do you play an instrument? If so, when, how often, and how long do you practice?

❖ Do you have guns? What are your beliefs about guns?

❖ Do you hunt? Fish? How often? How much time do you spend on it? What are your beliefs or feelings about hunting? Do you expect your partner to participate?

❖ How do you feel about gambling? Do you gamble? How often? Do you have a limit to how much money you are willing to gamble?

❖ How do you feel about nude sunbathing? Do you ever sunbathe nude? How do you feel about other nudist activities?

❖ Will you go shopping with your partner (for clothes, electronics, hardware, food, etc.)? Why or why not? How do you feel about it?

❖ Is there anything you do for entertainment that isn't discussed here (feed the ducks in a nearby lake, listen to readings at the local bookstore, etc.)?

OBSERVATIONS OF YOUR PARTNER

❖ Does your partner participate in your areas of interest?

❖ Does your partner's taste in television shows match your own? (Do they watch cartoons, soap operas, sports, horror movies, etc., to excess?) How does it affect your relationship?

❖ Do you feel your partner is too involved with any activity, e.g., reading, sports, television, gambling, shopping, going on-line, etc.? If so, how does it affect you?

❖ Does your partner participate in any activities that you'd really like to learn more about?

SELF-OBSERVATIONS

❖ Do you feel comfortable participating with your partner in the activities they enjoy?

❖ Have you discovered activities that you both love to do?

❖ Do you enjoy your partner's activities or merely tolerate them? Do any of them conflict with your core values?

❖ Does your partner participate in any activities that you cannot accept into your life? If so, how does that affect you?

✳

CHAPTER EIGHT

Morals, Values, Ethics, and Beliefs

hen Linda first met Alan, she didn't drink alcohol or eat meat. But after several years of being together, Linda suddenly realized that she had compromised on both matters. She found herself drinking on occasion and eating fish and chicken regularly, neither of which was okay with her. She realized, through self-observation, that she had wavered in her beliefs for the sake of convenience. Linda could not, however, blame Alan. She was responsible for her choices—both in partners and in her responses.

Since we tend to take on some of our partners' characteristics and lifestyles over time, it's wise to pay special attention to values and ethics. If you haven't done the Foreplay exercises in Chapter Two, go back and do them now; preparing those lists can serve as an excellent springboard for exploring the questions in this chapter.

These topics hit at the core of a person's being. Integrity, authenticity, and responsibility are key to being a healthy person in a healthy relationship. Watch to see whether the way your partner lives is in alignment with what they say. As a Native American friend says, "He sings a good song, but does he dance to it?" Be sure to ask the same question about yourself. We can change jobs, locations, partners, even physical features in this day and age, but the truth of who we are at heart follows us wherever we go. Consequently, it is important that your partner's "heart" is one you respect.

An interesting situation in Wendee and Steve's relationship is that they discovered quickly that a non-negotiable area of compatibility was that since they'd both been married before, neither of them wanted to get married again or have children. While they agreed on this, *Intellectual Foreplay* brought into view some related issues that they would not have thought to explore until they had become serious problems. When they came across a question about legal wills, they realized that in traditional relationships it is common for one partner to name the other partner in their will. In this case, however, Steve was planning to leave all his worldly belongings to a family member. Because the question was in the book, they were able to approach a topic that they wouldn't ordinarily have felt comfortable bringing up, and they have come to an understanding.

The value of *Intellectual Foreplay* is not just in discovering that someone is *compatible.* It is equally valuable in bringing *incompatibilities* to the forefront of the relationship, so that you can discuss them and make informed decisions. One woman in my class shared that as she grew up her father instilled in her the importance of security and legality. He emphasized things such as taxes and insurance. When she began dating a man who didn't pay taxes or have insurance, it was a major difficulty for her. While you may not see eye to eye on some of the topics in this chapter, if you let go of your need for control, you may find that your partner's perspective is good to know but won't affect the relationship. Other questions will reveal beliefs and attitudes that could deeply affect your well-being.

Values, morals, ethics, and beliefs, in general, are heavily influenced by our religious or spiritual affiliations. You'll find that some of the topics in this section regarding ghosts, miracles, etc., could easily be placed in the "Religion and Spirituality" chapter, as your spiritual beliefs certainly guide your perspective on these issues. I have placed them here, however, because there are other factors besides religion that influence these beliefs. See "Religion and Spirituality" for questions more specifically related to those topics.

Morals, values, ethics, and beliefs are often among the most uncompromising and non-negotiable areas of discussion. Watch for the little red flags! In one of my relationship classes, I asked students the question, "What rules do you live by?" Much to his wife's dismay, one man quickly shouted out, "Don't get caught!"

QUESTIONS TO ASK EACH PARTNER

❖ What are your values? What do you stand for?

❖ Do you have a personal set of rules that you live by (i.e., a code of ethics)? [See the Foreplay exercise below!]

❖ Are you honest? When is it appropriate not to be honest?

❖ How do you feel about your level of honesty?

❖ How do you define integrity?

❖ What is your level of integrity? How do you feel about your level of integrity?

❖ What would you fight for (literally and figuratively)?

❖ Arrange these values in order of importance to you: pleasure, wealth, love, power, knowledge, fame, spirituality.

❖ Arrange these values in order of importance to you: relationship, work, family, health, friends, hobbies.

❖ What are the most valuable lessons you've learned in life so far?

❖ When, if ever, is physical fighting appropriate (between any people, not just partners)?

❖ Would it ever be appropriate to strike or hit your partner?

❖ When, if ever, do you think stealing is appropriate? Have you ever stolen anything?

❖ When, if ever, do you think it's okay to break the law?

❖ If your partner wanted to go into a dangerous situation
for a just cause, would you support them in doing so?

❖ Whom do you idealize? Who are your heroes or heroines?

❖ What do you think the purpose of life is?
What do you think your life purpose is?

❖ What is your plan for fulfilling your life's purpose?

❖ What are the benefits or disadvantages of marriage/partnership
in fulfilling that purpose?

❖ What are your political views?

❖ Do you vote?

❖ How patriotic are you?

❖ Would you enlist in the military?

❖ Would you go to war? Have you been to war already?
If so, how did it affect you?

❖ What are your feelings about taxes? Do you pay them honestly?

❖ How do you feel about insurance? Do you have any?

❖ Are you an activist? About which issues are you adamant?

❖ How do you feel about fur coats or the use of animals for testing
or medical experiments?

❖ How do you feel about capital punishment?
Do you hold a strong position on it?

❖ How do you feel about abortion? Adoption?
   (Discuss specifically how these issues relate to your relationship.)

❖ What are your views and beliefs on feminism?

❖ What are your stereotypes about women? In what ways do you
   (or your partner) match them?

❖ What are your stereotypes about men? In what ways do you
   (or your partner) match them?

❖ Do you have any strict product loyalty, like only buying U.S.-made
   products, only Ford, only Macintosh, etc.? How do you feel about
   your partner having different preferences?

❖ Under what circumstances would you cross a picket line?

❖ What are your environmental views, and what are you personally
   willing to do about them?

❖ Do you believe in or actively practice recycling and conservation?

❖ How do you make decisions for yourself? Do you tend to be logical,
   intuitive, or indecisive?

❖ When you make decisions about your own life, do you take your
   partner into consideration?

❖ If you can see that you are wrong, do you hold onto your position
   anyway, or can you change your mind?

❖ Are you able to apologize for or take responsibility for your mistakes?
   Do you tend to blame others before accepting responsibility?

❖ In what ways is your age difference (or similarity) an issue? How does it affect entertainment choices, music preferences, cultural awareness, family, interests, beliefs, and future plans?

❖ Would you be willing to move to a place you don't want to live for money or a job opportunity? How about for your partner or family?

❖ Would you be willing to move if your spouse had a job opportunity somewhere else?

❖ Do you tend to trust people, or are you cautious or suspicious?

❖ Is it ever okay to lie? Under what conditions?

❖ Do you keep secrets? Is there anyone with whom you generally share all your secrets?

❖ Do you have a will? How do you feel about what happens to your belongings when you die?

❖ When you die, what are your wishes in terms of burial or cremation and funerals?

❖ Do you believe in donating organs? Are you listed as a donor?

❖ Do you believe in ghosts? Have you ever experienced a ghost?

❖ Has anything happened that made you believe in magic or miracles?

❖ Do you believe in U.F.O.s?

❖ Do you believe in astrology? What is your sign?

❖ Do you have any prejudices? How do they affect your life? Do you act on them?

❖ Are you comfortable with your personal level of morality?

❖ Do you live in alignment with what you say are your beliefs?

❖ In general, do you like people?

❖ In general, how do you treat people? How do you treat the homeless, other races, the poor; how do you react when someone asks you for something?

QUESTIONS TO EXPLORE AS A COUPLE

❖ As a couple, what are your main values and how do you prioritize them (the relationship, friends, family, money, hobbies, work, religion, etc.)?

❖ Who makes the decisions in the relationship?
Does one person have the final word?

❖ How are decisions that affect both partners handled?
If there is a difference of opinions, how is it decided?

❖ Are you able to disagree on your beliefs, political views, etc., and still get along?

OBSERVATIONS OF YOUR PARTNER

❖ Does your partner laugh at life or curse it?

❖ How does your partner treat other people?

❖ Does your partner live (and act) in alignment with what they say are their values, morals, and beliefs?

❖ Is your partner patient?

❖ Does your partner take responsibility for their actions or get defensive?

❖ Do you and your partner see yourselves in opposition
   or on the same team?

❖ Is your partner someone whom you want to become more like?
   In which ways? Are there ways you don't want to be more like them?

SELF-OBSERVATIONS

❖ Are you comfortable with your partner's apparent level of morality
   and integrity?

❖ Are you comfortable with the way decisions are handled within
   your relationship?

❖ Do you share or hold any ideals in common?

❖ Describe your perception of your partner.

❖ If your partner didn't do the Foreplay exercise on values identification
   in Chapter Two, ask yourself, after going through these questions,
   what you perceive your partner's values to be. How do they compare
   to your list of values?

 **Think about the rules that you live by, and generate your own personal
code of ethics. This may include things such as, "Respect your
elders," or "Do unto others as you would have them do unto you," or
"Honesty is the best policy." There may also be more subtle "rules" that you
believe in, such as, "The man should pay for everything," or "Children should be
seen, not heard." Spend some time identifying the rules that consciously and
unconsciously affect the way you live and your expectations of your partner.**

CHAPTER NINE

Commitment and Trust

ill and Tim were only able to get together on weekends due to the distance between their homes. Jill's schedule changed one week, and she decided to surprise Tim by showing up at his house one evening. She envisioned his romantic delight. When she was met less than enthusiastically, it pushed all her trust buttons. Tim claimed that he just didn't like surprises, but Jill felt sure that he was concealing something he didn't want her to find out about—such as his ex-girlfriend. She went ahead and stayed the night, but their relationship didn't last much longer. The lack of trust and commitment proved too great for them to endure.

Definitions of commitment and levels of fear around willingness and readiness to commit vary from person to person. Since trust, security, and safety are basic needs for most people, exploring your partner's beliefs and attitudes around these issues can be enlightening. Listen carefully to the answers. If your partner tells you early on that they are not ready for a relationship, believe them! People often tell the truth about their readiness or integrity at the very beginning of the relationship, but we usually don't listen, thinking we can overcome these obstacles. The problem is that the obstacles usually pop up again later, attached to an "I told you so way back when...." Pay special attention to what your partner does, in addition to what they say.

In today's world, there are a lot more variations in what are considered acceptable relationship practices. Polygamous relationships are written about in books and magazines; bisexual and gay relationships are becoming ever more common. There are also more divorced people in the dating market than ever before, many of whom have no intention of ever marrying again. Consequently, you may encounter partners whose attitudes and expectations about commitment vary greatly from your own.

Other variables you may encounter are differences in what constitutes "cheating." One person may feel that an occasional one-night stand is acceptable as long as it ends there, while another may feel that looking at adult magazines or Web sites is an infringement on the relationship. Attitudes can also change over time on issues such as these. First, clarify what a relationship and commitment mean to you, then explore and develop the concepts with your partner.

QUESTIONS TO ASK EACH PARTNER

❖ Are you involved with or seeing anyone else? Are you married?
   [Always a good one to ask early on!]

❖ What does love mean to you?

❖ Do you believe in "love at first sight"?

❖ What are your views on monogamy? Polygamy?

❖ Do you expect monogamy from your partner?

❖ Are you willing to be monogamous?

❖ What's the longest you've been monogamous in a relationship?

❖ Are you ready to be in a committed relationship?
   What does commitment mean to you?

❖ What's your biggest fear about making a commitment to someone?

❖ How do you feel about living together?

❖ What are the advantages and disadvantages of getting married instead of living together?

❖ What are the advantages and disadvantages of living together instead of (or before) marriage? Are those the same for both partners?

❖ If you're planning to live with your partner before marriage, how long do you intend to wait before marrying?

❖ How long should an engagement last?

❖ If you were to get married, in what ways, if any, do you think it would change the relationship?

❖ What do you think marriage means?

❖ Have you been married before? If so, how long were you married? How do you think that experience has influenced your present feelings about marriage?

❖ Why haven't you been married before, or why aren't you still married?

❖ Why do you want to get married, or why don't you want to get married?

❖ What do you want out of marriage: a lover, a housekeeper, a cook, a provider, a handyman, a companion, a friend, etc.?

❖ What is your view of divorce? What do you consider "valid" reasons for getting a divorce?

❖ What does trust mean to you?

❖ Are you trustworthy?

❖ Do you tend to trust until given a reason not to, or do you distrust until trust has been proven?

❖ How long do you think it takes to build trust?

❖ What does it take to rebuild trust after it's been damaged? Can it be rebuilt?

❖ How do you feel about your partner talking to, looking at, or flirting with members of the opposite sex (or same sexual orientation)? How would you handle it?

❖ How do you feel about your partner greeting members of the opposite sex (or same sexual orientation) with a hug or a kiss?

❖ If infidelity or attraction to another person is experienced, should it be discussed with your partner, concealed, or ignored?

❖ How do you handle temptation?

❖ What do you think you would do if your partner were unfaithful?

❖ Is it okay for your partner to ask you where you've been? With whom? Doing what?

❖ Have you ever snooped or played detective (read your partner's letters or journals; looked in pockets, purses, or wallets; pushed redial on the phone when you came home, etc.)?

❖ If your partner had an affair, would you want to know about it?

❖ Do you tend to be jealous? What makes you jealous?

❖ How possessive do you consider yourself?

❖ What is your level of fear around being betrayed?
What would you consider a betrayal?

❖ Do you believe that a relationship requires hard work,
or that it should be easy?

❖ Are you willing to work on making the relationship better?

❖ Would you be willing to get counseling if there were unresolved
issues between you and your partner?

❖ Do you tend to think in a long-term or short-term way
about relationships?

❖ Do you think in terms of "we" or "I"?

❖ Are you willing to make changes for your partner or the relationship?

❖ Do you prefer a relationship that is steady and consistent or
one that is full of drama and changes in intensity?

❖ How do you feel about your partner showing up at your
home unexpectedly?

❖ What do you think your level of commitment would be in the
following situations:

> If your partner got cancer and had to have a breast or testicle
> removed?

> If your partner had any terminal illness or a stroke, or had to
> have a limb amputated or all their teeth pulled?

> If your partner lost their job or had their income reduced?

> If your partner became significantly overweight or underweight?

> If your partner was arrested or put in jail?

If you found out your partner was sterile or infertile?

If your partner had an affair?

OBSERVATIONS OF YOUR PARTNER

❖ Does your partner look at other men or women? If so, do you mind?

❖ Is your partner flirtatious? How do you feel about it?

❖ How possessive do you consider your partner?

❖ How does your partner treat you when they are feeling jealous/possessive?

❖ How does your partner react when you are jealous or possessive?

❖ Does your partner ever embarrass you in public?

SELF-OBSERVATIONS

❖ Do you trust your partner?

❖ Do you feel ready to commit to a relationship? To this relationship? Are you already emotionally committed to your partner?

❖ Do you ever fear that right after you make a serious commitment, the "real right person" for you will come along, but you won't be available?

❖ Are you honest about what you think and do? Do you accept the consequences for those choices, or are you more likely to conceal your actions if you've done something wrong?

CHAPTER TEN

Romance

 bout a month before we got married, Steven was busy with something in the back yard that he wouldn't let me see. A short while later, he came in with a scruffy but cute teddy bear that some dog had unceremoniously deposited in the yard. When Steven found the bear, it was filthy and had been torn apart. He rescued it, scrubbed it clean and sewed it back together, and then gave it to me as a gift. Steven is a very masculine kind of guy. Thus, for him to do something so tender—something that I would have thought somewhat "out of character"—was one of the most romantic moments in our relationship.

Webster's defines romance as "a tendency of mind toward the wonderful and mysterious, something belonging rather to fiction than to everyday life." Romance is the stuff that makes your relationship seem special rather than mundane. It is the juice that makes you feel that you are the prince and princess in a fairy tale—but the "spell" is easily broken if you don't both pay attention to honoring this "royalty" in the other. No one wants to wake up one day and realize that the loving relationship they yearned for is finally here and all it really boils down to is slave labor. It is each partner's responsibility to keep the essence alive, to let the other know that you honor them as a sweetheart—not just as a parent to your children or housekeeper or handyman, but as your beloved…someone wonderful and mysterious.

Romance can be addictive. It's often poured on in the beginning of a relationship, and just when you're hooked, it can stop. Yet there are ways that it can be kept alive. Exploring each other's wants and "needs" and keeping the romance alive simply make life a lot more fun! Keeping the romance going in a relationship over the course of time may come naturally to some, but for others it requires conscious effort. It is easy to slip into a day-to-day routine that doesn't include spending a moment to watch the sunset or asking your partner to climb up on the roof to watch a meteor shower at two in the morning or to kiss under the full moon. To me, honoring all that is wonderful and mysterious in life *is* romantic. Moments in nature, sharing the silence of a canyon, a campfire in the backyard, watching waves break by moonlight, seeing fireflies dance in the trees, making time to honor the magical things of life and sharing them with your sweetheart—these are moments to live for! To you, romance may mean taking a moment to do that special thing for your partner that they like so much, that perhaps you could take or leave, but doing it anyway because you know it matters to them.

While it may seem that talking about what you want takes some of the mystery out of the romance—kind of like having to ask someone to tell you that they love you—the challenge is that if you don't discuss it, you may consistently miss the mark. Because romance means being outdoors to one person and it means wearing sexy nightgowns to another and it means bringing flowers to another or wearing cologne to someone else, it is way too easy not to honor your partner's sense of romance—and not to *be* honored.

People also experience love in different ways, which are helpful to know about. Some people respond best to visual stimulation—feeling loved when someone takes the time to present concrete, visible signs of affection. Other people are kinesthetic and need to be touched to feel loved. Others are auditory and need to hear how their partner feels about them.

Tiffany, being visual and auditory, spent hours cleaning house, set a beautiful table, and prepared a special meal to let her husband know how much she loved him. She anxiously waited for him to come home so he could *see* what she had done and so she could *hear* his appreciation and love. When he arrived, however, Jack said nothing about the house or table setting but immediately wanted to sweep Tiffany off her feet, take her upstairs, and make love with her to show her how much he cared. Instead of either partner feeling honored, both felt rejected. Tiffany was upset that Jack hadn't noticed anything she had done and consequently was less than receptive to his attempts at lovemaking. He thought he was trying to *give* something to her, while she thought he was trying to *get* something from her. She felt unappreciated, and he was totally baffled. While you don't have to have the same means of experiencing love, knowing each partner's style can help tremendously.

A note about these questions: Turn to the "Holidays" chapter for questions about the celebration of romantic holidays such as Valentine's Day and anniversaries. Questions regarding gifts are also in "Holidays"; however, since gift-giving is often a significant part of romance and dating, it should also be considered here.

QUESTIONS TO ASK EACH PARTNER

❖ Define what romance means to you.

❖ How important is romance to you?

❖ Do you believe that romance is different than sex?
   If so, describe that difference.

❖ In what ways do you consider yourself to be a romantic person?

❖ What are your expectations around romance?

❖ What would you consider a perfect date?

❖ Do you think it's important to continue romance after marriage?
   If so, how would you do it?

❖ How would you create a romantic mood? How would you do it six months into a relationship? Ten years into a relationship?

❖ Do you believe in going on "dates" together, even after marriage?

❖ Do you nurture your partner through massage or nonsexual touch?

❖ Do you like to be nurtured through massage or nonsexual touch?

❖ How do you let your partner know that you want to have an intimate evening?

❖ Are you publicly affectionate? To what degree?

❖ Are you comfortable with public affection? To what degree?

❖ How do you perceive that you are loved?
How do you like to be appreciated?

❖ Are you comfortable saying the words, "I love you"?

❖ Do you need to *hear* that your partner loves you to feel loved? How frequently?

❖ Do you need to be touched by your partner to feel loved?

❖ How do you feel about pet names like "Honey," "Sweetheart," "Baby," etc. (at home and in public)?

❖ How do you refer to or introduce your partner (husband/wife, boyfriend/girlfriend, old lady/old man, etc.)? How do you want to be referred to?

❖ Are you able to be playful with your partner?

❖ Are there any places that feel romantic to you?

Observations of Your Partner

❖ How does your partner respond when you touch them?
In public? In private?

❖ How important do you think romance is to your partner?

❖ How does your partner communicate love and appreciation for you?
Are you comfortable with that expression?

Self-Observations

❖ Are you satisfied with the current level of romance in your
relationship?

❖ Do you feel passionate about your partner?

❖ How do you show love and appreciation to your partner?
Do you tell your partner verbally? Show them physically? Buy gifts?

**Assess what you each consider to be romantic, write the ideas down,
and compare your lists. Even if your lists aren't the same, make a conscious effort to include items from each list in your daily life, and participate in these activities with genuine enthusiasm. If you don't have a partner,
honor yourself—buy yourself flowers, or take yourself to the beach at sunset!**

**Take turns crafting "the perfect date," or describing romantic places,
and generate a list that you can use to stimulate romance and fun in
your relationship.**

CHAPTER ELEVEN

Religion
and Spirituality

ne couple, Sid and Jessica, began dating regularly. As they engaged in the *Intellectual Foreplay* of their relationship, it soon became obvious that they had encountered a barrier. Jessica was devoted to a very strict religious order and attended meetings several times a week. Sid, also devout, was raised in an Eastern philosophy and had since developed a personal relationship with God that didn't include going to church indoors. Jessica kept inviting Sid to church, which he repeatedly declined—much to her disappointment. It was evident that neither would change their deeply adhered-to ways for the other, nor could either fully respect the other's lifestyle without judgment. Although they were compatible in many other ways, the impending challenges of merging social lives, raising children, dealing with judgment-and-control issues were just too great.

Isn't religion one of the topics we're supposed to avoid (along with politics)? People's religious beliefs are often so deeply held as *the truth* that it is often a difficult area in which to find compromise. Throughout history, interreligious marriages and relationships have been as difficult for society and families to accept as interracial relationships. Fortunately, the world is becoming a more aware and accepting place; however, differences in religious beliefs and practices can still bring huge challenges.

A primary issue here is that often, if you and your partner were raised in different belief systems, one of you may be "going to Hell" in the other's beliefs. There are a lot of problems love and understanding can conquer, but "going to Hell" isn't one of them!

Religious beliefs are often so strong and so narrow that it is definitely helpful for the relationship if you are of like mind. I once had a partner tell me he loved me "in spite of my religion." Since, in my mind, my spirituality is the essence of who I am, his mere tolerance of this aspect of me foreshadowed serious and deep issues that were yet to come between us. Since primary values are often instilled in us through our religious or spiritual upbringing, people are more likely to be aligned in their values if their religious beliefs are aligned.

Finding a partner with the same belief system will surely make your relationship easier, and it will also assist you in following your spiritual path. However, differences of belief can be lived with and even help you thrive if you are both open-minded enough to accept the other's right to their beliefs or if you can take the best of both beliefs and come up with some common ground. The starting point for this process is to enter into discussion and find out as much as you can about where the other stands. Keep in mind that how spiritually people *live* can actually speak more loudly and importantly than what they *say* or what name they assign to their belief system. You may find that even though you call your beliefs by different names, you live spiritually in the exact same ways.

QUESTIONS TO ASK EACH PARTNER

❖ Do you believe in God? What are your religious beliefs and views about God?

❖ What, if any, religion do you follow? Do you read, believe in, or follow any particular spiritual writings or leaders?

❖ In what ways do you practice your beliefs?

❖ What belief system were you raised in, and does it differ from the one you have now?

❖ Do you live in a community where you receive support for
   your religious beliefs or are condemned for them?

❖ Do you see a difference between religion and spirituality?
   If so, is one more important to you than the other?

❖ To what degree does religion or spirituality play a role in your life?
   In your work?

❖ In what ways do you seek out spiritual growth?

❖ In your priorities, where does spiritual growth fit in?
   How important is it to you?

❖ Do you pray? If so, do you ask for things, give thanks, or both?
   Do you believe God hears you? Answers you?

❖ Are you afraid of God? Why or why not?

❖ Were you afraid of God as a child?

❖ Do you think God is male or female? Neither? Both?

❖ What are your beliefs about evil? Do you believe in the devil?

❖ How important is it to you that your partner has spiritual goals,
   rituals, and beliefs?

❖ How important is it to you to share your spiritual practices
   with your partner?

❖ What kind of time is involved in your religious practices
   (e.g., going to church, meetings, workshops, meditating, etc.)?

❖ Do you say grace before meals? Are you willing to?
Who says grace? What do you say?

❖ Does a certain day of the week have a special meaning to you
(Sunday, for example)? Do you do anything different on that day?

❖ How important is religion to your family? To your partner's family?
Does this affect your relationship? Would your family welcome your
partner if they were of a different religion?

❖ What do you see as the role of religion in marriage, and what is the
role of marriage in your religion?

❖ How do you feel about metaphysics? New-age thought?

❖ What do you think about E.S.P. (extrasensory perception)
or psychic abilities?

❖ Have you ever had psychic experiences?

❖ Do you believe in an "Inner Wisdom" or a sense of intuition that
allows you to hear divine guidance? If so, do you have a sense of
access to yours?

❖ Do you believe in guardian angels or guiding spirits?

❖ Is there anything you could be shown or told that would make you
change your present spiritual beliefs? Would you change your religion
to match your partner's?

❖ Are there any beliefs or spiritual practices in your partner's religion
that you absolutely cannot accept or respect (no blood transfusions or
medical help, no celebrating holidays, no birth control, reincarnation,
narrow-minded thought, open-minded thought, etc.)? Can you
resolve these differences?

❖ If you're planning to have children, how will you raise them spiritually?

❖ What stereotypes do you believe about different religions?

❖ Are there any physical places where you feel closer to God?
   Where would you go to find tranquillity, solitude, or a connection
   to a Higher Power?

❖ How accepting are you of people with religious views different than
   your own? Do you think they are wrong or just different? Do you
   think they are doomed, ignorant, entitled to their own beliefs, etc.?

❖ What are your beliefs about what happens after death?

❖ How do you feel about death? Does it scare you?

QUESTIONS TO EXPLORE AS A COUPLE

❖ Are there major or seriously conflicting spiritual beliefs between
   you and your partner? Even if specific beliefs differ, do you each
   value spirituality to a similar degree?

❖ Do you feel you and your partner are on the same path?
   Do you feel you can reach your spiritual goals within this relationship?

❖ Is it okay with each partner for the other one to have their own beliefs?

❖ If your religious beliefs differ, how will your union be viewed by
   your families?

OBSERVATIONS OF YOUR PARTNER

❖ Do your partner's beliefs and behaviors appear to be in alignment?
Does what they say match what they do?

SELF-OBSERVATIONS

❖ Do you respect your partner's spiritual beliefs?

❖ Do you feel that your partner respects your beliefs?

✳

CHAPTER TWELVE

Health

O ne man whom I dated had a mother who was a hypochondriac and constantly complained that she was ill. I didn't know this, so I was shocked when she told us that she needed to go to the hospital and he showed no concern. He then explained to me that she had "needed to go to the hospital" for no apparent reason his whole life. What I didn't realize was how this experience with his mother would impact me—and our relationship—when I got sick. The first sign of a cold or flu met with zero understanding. Whenever I was sick as a child, I always received the sweet care of my mother and her cool hands on my hot forehead. The shock of receiving no care or concern in a relationship was just too much of a contrast. While I didn't expect my partner to be a full-time caretaker, I did expect compassion. How you and your partner treat each other when you are sick is an important consideration.

If you plan to "live happily-ever-after" with someone, it helps if you are both "living happily" in the first place. Being healthy in mind and body contributes greatly to that happiness. If you enjoy an active lifestyle, but your potential partner does not, it could eventually impact the quality of your time together. Even more important to your relationship than actual health or handicaps, however, may be attitude. You may simply be looking for someone whom you trust will make the most of what they have got— continuing to embrace life in spite of their physical challenges.

Health issues are very personal, and your level of comfort with a partner's health is also very individual. "In sickness and in health" is a vow that carries with it a responsibility. Once again, knowing yourself is important. If you find a potential partner with health issues, honestly assess yourself to determine how able you are to handle the situation. Do you and your partner have the means to hire help if necessary or to get adequate treatment? Are you a caregiver by nature—and will you need to be? Will you be able to stay with your partner through their times of need? Health issues certainly don't need to "disqualify" a wonderful partner; it is inevitable that we all will have health challenges at some point. However, as you choose to get involved with someone, self-observe and, based on your present levels of information, assess your willingness and ability to "tough out" potential difficulties and variances in health with them.

A particular challenge to relationships is a major unforeseen change in a partner's health. It is very difficult to know how we would respond to an event such as this, especially at the beginning of a relationship. Although there is no way to foresee what could happen, reasonable measures of preventative medicine to maintain health can be taken. If you have health challenges, be aware of how your moods may impact your partner and the relationship. Pay attention to the frequency of your illnesses, to your expectations of your partner when you are sick, and your willingness to do what you can to heal.

One man, Jerry, shared with us that he had a challenge in a past relationship determining how much of his fiancée, Keri's, extreme mood swings were related to physical health and how much her claims of hormonal imbalance were just an excuse for being mean. He pointed out that a valid question in the arena of health is to consider how much a person is willing to take responsibility for recognizing how their mental and physical health is impacting their lives and to seek appropriate professional help for fixing the problem. Keri justified her temper by blaming a physical condition, but she didn't adequately work to resolve the problem. It ultimately led to the end of their engagement.

Another health-related issue is alcohol and substance abuse. This is one of the most common problems in relationships as well as one filled with denial. Addressing the issue before you are seriously involved can save you a lot of drama. Begin with self-observation of your own behavior and consider yourself *as a partner.* Do you have any potentially troublesome substance-use problems or addictions? Then turn your attention to your partner's substance use and addictions. Remember that what appears to be occasional drinking on a date can become intolerable on an everyday basis.

If alcohol and/or other substances are a part of your life, you can be guaranteed that they are interfering with your relationships. Anything that regularly alters your perspective, your decisions, your communication, or your health—and/or costs money—will affect your relationships. If you are involved with someone who regularly uses drugs or alcohol, look at your own co-dependency issues and think long and hard about what you are choosing to accept. Are you dependent on your partner's substance use? Are there unconscious benefits to you in having a partner who is using? One couple, Dave and Tina, encountered an interesting challenge when she decided to stop using drugs and alcohol. Tina was suddenly afraid to make love with her husband because she realized that in the fifteen years that they had been together, they had never made love without being under the influence of some substance. This made it very tempting for her to go back to what was comfortable—and for him to encourage her to—but they managed to overcome the fear and embrace a new phase in their relationship.

When it comes to dealing with a partner's substance abuse, negotiation for change seldom works, at least not until rock bottom has been hit and ultimatums are offered—and sometimes not even then. Accepting these behaviors in your life is seldom a choice that leads to a healthy outcome. Resisting your partner's behavior will only cause drama and struggle between you. Consider your options and decide carefully whether to enter or stay in a relationship in which your life is in the hands of addiction.

In our youth, it is easy to take health for granted, but as we age—and endure time together—the inevitability of having to deal with health issues becomes imminent. When you get involved with someone considerably older than you, your willingness to deal with their age-related health issues must also be considered. There are safety issues embedded in the topic of health as well. Fears of abandonment at our greatest time of need and the vulnerability of needing assistance are both issues that can emerge as we age or face health problems. Differences of opinion about what is appropriate health care—and timeliness of care—also need to be discussed. Once again, keep in mind that these questions are not intended to find out what is "wrong" with the other person. Many of these things are just wise to know about your partner, so that you can adequately assist them if the need arises or in the case of an emergency.

A more extensive look at issues related to aging can be found in the chapter on "Future." Mental-health issues are primarily found in Chapter Four, which addresses self-esteem and emotions. Questions addressing HIV/AIDS and sexually transmitted diseases are in the "Sex" chapter.

QUESTIONS TO ASK EACH PARTNER

❖ Do you feel healthy?

❖ How comfortable are you with your present level of health?

❖ Do you take care of yourself through exercise, rest, and diet? Is there anything you would like to do differently?

❖ Does your health ever stop you from doing any activities?

❖ What do you do for exercise?

❖ How do you feel about exercise?

❖ How much time do you spend getting exercise?

❖ How important is it to you that your partner exercises?

❖ How do you feel if your partner does not like your preferred activities? Is it okay for them to say no?

❖ Are you a member of a health club? Are you willing/interested in joining a health club?

❖ How often are you sick?

❖ Have you ever had any serious illnesses?

❖ Do you have asthma, diabetes, or any other health condition?

❖ When you are sick, do you like to be pampered or left alone? What do you expect of your partner when you are sick?

❖ If your partner were to get sick, how willing to nurse them or take care of them do you think you would be? How would you feel about providing care during a long-term or chronic illness?

❖ Do you have special dietary requirements?

❖ Do you eat for emotional reasons? If so, which emotional situations cause you to eat?

❖ Have you ever been bulimic or anorexic?

❖ Do you have allergies? If so, how do they affect you?

❖ How often do you go to doctors?

❖ Do you have any problem with getting shots, blood tests, going to the dentist, etc.?

❖ Do you have health insurance? Do you believe in health insurance?

❖ Do you have life insurance? Do you believe in life insurance?

❖ How do you feel about taking medicines? Natural remedies?

❖ How do you feel about taking vitamins? Do you take them?

❖ Are you allergic to any medicines?

❖ What, if any, illnesses or inheritable problems run in your family, such as mongoloidism, diabetes, cystic fibrosis, heart disease, or sickle-cell anemia?

❖ How do you feel about preventative medications, such as vaccinations and flu shots?

❖ How much time/money/energy do you put into preventative efforts (massage, exercise, diet, health clubs, etc.)?

❖ How much time/money/energy do you put into cures (doctors' visits, medicines, healers, etc.)?

❖ FOR WOMEN: How are you affected by your periods and PMS? Menopause? In what ways do these issues impact your relationships? How long do your periods and PMS last? What measures do you take to relieve the symptoms and minimize their impact on your life/relationships?

❖ Do you believe that there is any connection between a person's emotional health and physical health?

❖ Do you believe in the mind's ability to heal?

❖ Have you ever been trained in C.P.R. or first aid?

❖ Do you tend to be accident-prone?

❖ Have you ever broken any bones or had any surgeries?

❖ Are you addicted to anything (drugs, food, alcohol, cigarettes, coffee, sex, exercise, etc.)? If so, how do these addictions affect your relationships?

❖ Do you smoke (or chew tobacco)? In what situations? How much? How often?

❖ If you smoke, how do you feel when someone asks you not to in their presence?

❖ Do you drink? In what situations? How much? How often?

❖ Do you use illegal drugs? If so, what kind? In what situations? How much? How often?

❖ Are you willing to stop or reduce your use of drugs, alcohol, or cigarettes for the sake of your health or the health of your relationship?

❖ What are you like when under the influence of drugs or alcohol?

❖ What is your limit on driving and drinking? At what point do you designate a driver, get a cab, etc.? (Or do you?)

QUESTIONS TO EXPLORE AS A COUPLE

❖ Do you or your partner have any health problems that could affect each other or your relationship?

❖ Do you exercise together or independently? Do you like it that way?

❖ Do you *have* to work out together, or can one of you opt not to?

❖ Are you each in charge of your own health, or does one of you push the other to behave in healthier ways?

❖ How do drugs and alcohol impact your relationship? If either or both were totally removed from the relationship, how would it change things?

OBSERVATIONS OF YOUR PARTNER

❖ Does your partner take care of himself/herself physically? Are they healthy? Do they take responsibility for healing or for their attitude in terms of accepting or coping with illness or disability?

❖ How supportive is your partner when you are sick?

❖ Does your or your partner's use of drugs and/or alcohol have an effect on the relationship?

❖ What is your partner like under the influence of drugs and/or alcohol? How do they treat you when they are under the influence?

❖ If your partner smokes, how respectful are they of others who do not?

❖ How comfortable does your partner seem to be with their body?

SELF-OBSERVATIONS

❖ How comfortable are you with your body and level of health?

❖ Are there patterns to when you tend to get sick?

❖ How comfortable are you with your partner's health?

❖ How supportive are you when your partner is sick?

※

CHAPTER THIRTEEN

Time

I used to date a man who kept me waiting all the time. We would agree on when we were to meet, but when I showed up, he would still have an hour more of this and that to do. This went on for years, and I felt that his lack of consideration was indicative of his sense that my time—*and thus my life*—was not as important as his. At that time, my self-esteem wasn't healthy enough for me to stop accepting this treatment. When we value ourselves and our time first, it is much more likely that others will also recognize our value.

How we choose to spend our time is what we choose to do with our lives. Punctuality, procrastination, and similarity in scheduling can have a huge impact on compatibility if respect isn't an underlying value. While one person may feel they should do everything with their partner, another may feel that that is too much and want time with other people or alone. How your partner treats time can give you a lot of information on their attitude about life.

Beliefs about and approaches to time management range from "fashionably late" to extreme attention to punctuality. Some people set their clocks ahead to give them an extra buffer, while others adamantly set their clocks with precision. Some use day planners, while others just wing it. Although style differences are interesting to note, as long as both partners have a system that works for them, take responsibility for themselves, and are respectful of their partners, time-management differences don't have to impact the relationship. It is when the system doesn't work or when we try to convert our partners to our way that challenges can arise.

QUESTIONS TO ASK EACH PARTNER

❖ How much time do you think a couple should spend together?

❖ How much time do you like to spend alone?

❖ What is a *typical* day like for you in terms of time schedules?

❖ What would your *ideal* day be like in terms of time schedules?

❖ Does your daily routine tend to be flexible or rigid?

❖ Do you tend to be punctual (on time) or late to events?

❖ How do you manage your time?

❖ Do you make lists of tasks or things to do? Do you follow them?

❖ Do you feel you use time well, waste time, or procrastinate? Does this vary with different moods or activities?

❖ Are you ever spontaneous, or do you need to plan things in advance? How do you handle it when plans unexpectedly change?

❖ How do you feel about wearing a watch?

❖ Do you set watches and clocks fast or at the actual time?

❖ Do you make plans *with* your partner or *for* your partner?

❖ How much time do you spend on the phone with family or friends? Business associates?

❖ How much time do you devote to work each day? Do you often work in the evenings or on weekends?

❖ What do you consider quality time?

❖ What do you consider a waste of time?

❖ Under what circumstances do you tend to feel bored?

❖ How do you like to spend your free time? Together? Alone?

QUESTIONS TO EXPLORE AS A COUPLE

❖ Are you satisfied with the amount of time you spend together?

❖ Are you satisfied with the quality of time you spend together?

❖ Does one of you like more time alone than the other? If so, how do you work that out?

❖ Are your work schedules compatible?

OBSERVATIONS OF YOUR PARTNER

❖ Is your partner spontaneous? Do you like that?

❖ Is your partner respectful and considerate of your time?

Self-Observations

❖ When you are apart, do you think about your partner?
  Do you think about what they are doing at that particular time?

❖ In general, how does your partner's use of time affect you and your
  relationship (i.e., is there a sense of being rushed and out of time or a
  "We'll get to it tomorrow" attitude)?

❖ Are you respectful of your partner's time?

✳

PART THREE

Where Did You Come From?

PAST

FAMILY

FRIENDS

EDUCATION
AND INTELLIGENCE

CHAPTER FOURTEEN

Past

W hen I talked with Wendee and Steve about their experience with *Intellectual Foreplay,* Steve confessed that he didn't want to tell Wendee the truth on certain questions about his past for fear that she wouldn't like him. He managed to observe himself and acknowledge this feeling, and opted to tell her the truth. He realized that if he told her the truth and she turned away, it was better to find out early on. If he told lies and she stayed, he would always have to worry that someday she would find out the truth. As it turned out, the truth was okay with her. The value of sharing the deepest and darkest about yourself with your partner and being accepted cannot be overvalued. It is the experience of unconditional love.

Many of us have a hard time leaving our past behind. We bring with us into our present lives and relationships our experiences, memories, habits, fears, and, hopefully, lessons learned. Knowledge of the past can be very useful as a tool for understanding certain situations or behaviors. It can also be, however, a fairly vulnerable area to open up to a partner. Trust is a necessary ingredient in every relationship. If you have an intuitive feeling that you are unsafe sharing certain aspects of your past with your partner, honor that feeling. However, in addition to honoring your feeling, pay close attention to the feeling and what it may tell you about your relationship. This feeling is information. Why do you feel unsafe? Is it because you don't trust your partner's response or want their approval? Rather than just not sharing, let your partner know what you're feeling. Their response is also information. Along these same lines, remember that if you withhold important events, beliefs, or experiences, your partner may fall in love with an *illusion,* with what you want them to believe, instead of with *you.* This may work for a while, but invariably your "true colors" will show through later.

Some rules for exploring the past together can help. One rule is to promise *never* to throw past mistakes in the other person's face. Another is to be careful not to judge past actions harshly, because we all change and grow. It is from our mistakes that we learn. A person's beliefs and behaviors *now* are far more important than what has happened before. The catch is that because our basic ways of being and our deep-rooted belief systems can show up in past actions, examining the past can be valuable. The purpose of these questions, however, is not so that you can judge or criticize your partner and what is right for *them,* but rather to determine what is right for *you.* Another rule is to ask and answer only those questions that are relevant to your relationship and share only those experiences that help you know each other. This is not about "digging up the dirt." This is about getting to know each other in a deep, meaningful, and honest way.

It is often a challenge to get present in relationships—to see what *is* rather than what *was.* Tony found, when he got involved with Deena, that she constantly accused him of cheating because of what her old boyfriend did. Her fear of being treated the same way was carried into their relationship, even though Tony wasn't cheating. By talking about what you are feeling and being honest with each other, you will be better able to release the past.

A note on these questions: if you're interested in asking about the current role of past partners, turn to the "Friends" chapter.

QUESTIONS TO ASK EACH PARTNER

❖ Describe your life and its major events. In which ways does your past affect you now?

❖ Describe yourself as a child. What was your childhood like?

❖ Describe yourself as a teenager.

❖ What are your favorite or most vivid childhood memories?

❖ What has been your favorite age or time period in your life so far?

❖ Do you feel you were treated fairly as a child? Elaborate.

❖ What were your major sources of joy growing up?

❖ What were your main worries or concerns? Areas of sadness?

❖ Were you named after someone? Do you like your name? Does it have a special meaning?

❖ When you were a child or teenager, whom could you go to with your problems?

❖ Did you ever run away from home? If so, how come and where did you go?

❖ Is there any history of physical, sexual, or emotional abuse in your family?

❖ Have you ever been abandoned or physically, emotionally, or sexually abused? If so, how have you coped with it? How does this impact your current relationships?

❖ Is there any one person who had a strong, positive influence on you when you were a child?

❖ Is there any one person who had a negative influence on you when you were a child?

❖ Who was your hero or heroine when you were a child?

❖ What was your economic level when you were a child?

❖ Is there any part of your life you wish you could re-do or undo?

❖ Is there any part of your life you enjoyed so much that you wish you could live it again?

❖ How long ago was your last relationship?

❖ In general, were your past relationships positive or negative experiences?

❖ Have there been recurring problems in your past relationships? If so, what were they?

❖ What lessons have you learned from each relationship you've been in?

❖ Do you see any patterns in your old relationships, partners, or behavior? If so, how do you feel these patterns affect you now?

❖ How do you feel about keeping pictures and love letters from past relationships? How do you feel about your partner keeping them?

❖ Have you ever been arrested? Do you have a criminal record? If so, what were the circumstances? How does this affect your life now? Is the law after you for anything now?

❖ Have you ever been hospitalized for mental illness or stress? If so, what were the circumstances?

❖ Have you ever been violent? In what situations, if any, do you become violent?

❖ Have you ever been treated violently? If so, what happened?

❖ Has anyone ever committed a major crime against you (e.g., theft, robbery, assault, rape, etc.)? If so, what were the circumstances, and how has it affected you?

❖ Are there certain issues from your past that are of particular concern to you (trust, substance abuse, abandonment) or that affect your current relationships?

❖ Have you ever had counseling? Are you getting counseling now? Would you be willing to get counseling if your past was getting in your way?

Questions to Explore as a Couple

❖ Have you shared your past with each other through photographs?

❖ Are you comfortable sharing your past with each other?

Observations of Your Partner

❖ Does your partner appear to have any past "baggage," resentments, or experiences that get in the way of healthy relationships?

❖ Does your partner tend to accuse you of behaviors that a past partner did?

❖ Does your partner's past affect you (consider past spouses, children, legal issues, trust issues, abuse issues…)?

SELF-OBSERVATIONS

❖ Are you keeping any secrets that may someday affect your partner's life or your relationship?

❖ Is there anything you feel shame or remorse about from your past?

❖ Is there anything you're holding onto that still needs healing?

❖ Are there any deaths or losses that you are still grieving from your past?

✳

CHAPTER FIFTEEN

Family

ynn comes from a very close family and calls home several times a week to speak with them. When she got involved with Barry, she was surprised that he wouldn't call home even on Father's Day. After trying for years to get Barry to be more communicative with his family, she realized that she wasn't accepting his situation or allowing him to follow his own path and learn his own lessons. On his side, it was hard for him to understand why she needed to talk to her family so often. When they both stopped trying to make one person right and the other wrong and just allowed each other their own styles, their relationship thrived.

We hear so much nowadays about how our "dysfunctional" families can affect us as adults. Families can affect a relationship not only in terms of the individual's behavior, but also in terms of the future. This, of course, varies, but even though there is no sure way to know the ultimate effect, a potential partner's family relationships can tell us a lot about what may show up down the line, or they can simply help to explain current behavior and belief systems. How close each partner is to their family, how much time they spend together, whether you are compatible with your partner's family, and whether they accept you can all have tremendous impacts on the success of the relationship.

We've heard many stories of how parents/in-laws broke up relationships with their disapproval and involvement. In some cases, the parents' disapproval is grounded in legitimate concern, as it may be that they are in a better position to view the relationship objectively. It may also be that the parents' values differ so greatly from those of the partner's that the relationship separates the family, rather than the other way around.

This is another arena in which you have to practice acceptance. Resisting who your partner is and how they relate to their family will not serve anyone. Review your choices and recognize that if you choose to accept your partner, you are also accepting, to some degree, a relationship with their family.

QUESTIONS TO ASK EACH PARTNER

❖ Describe your relationship with your family.

❖ What is the make-up of your family (divorced parents, deceased, stepfamilies, etc.)?

❖ What is your ethnic or cultural background?

❖ Does your partner's cultural background matter to you?
Does it matter to your and your partner's families?

❖ Are there cultural or family practices or traditions that affect the relationship? If so, how?

❖ What is your birth order in the family?

❖ Were you close to your brothers/sisters as a child? Now?

❖ Are your parents/siblings/grandparents still alive?

❖ Describe your mother. In what ways are you like her?

❖ Describe your father. In what ways are you like him?

❖ How do your parents treat each other? Describe their relationship.

❖ What is the best thing your parents did for you (or taught you), either individually or together?

❖ How often do you contact your family (phone, letters, visits)?

❖ To your knowledge, were your parents faithful to each other? How did that affect you and your beliefs about marriage?

❖ Did your parents stay married? Did your parents ever divorce or separate?

❖ Are you proud of your family or embarrassed by them?

❖ Do you feel it's necessary to ask your partner before friends and family come over (if you're living together)?

❖ How is your family's relationship with extended family (i.e., grandparents, aunts, uncles, cousins, etc.)?

❖ How does (or did) your family deal with conflict?

❖ Are there any family members to whom you no longer speak or with whom you have a limited relationship? If so, why? Do you want to heal the relationship? How has it affected you?

❖ Who makes (or made) the decisions in your family?

❖ How did your parents discipline you? How do you feel about that method?

❖ What kinds of rules did you have in your household as a child?

❖ Is there anything you wish had been different in the way you were parented/raised?

❖ How do your parents treat you?

❖ As your parents age, what kind of responsibility do you expect to take on? Would you need/want to move closer to them? What about aging brothers and sisters?

❖ Would you take in a parent or relative if they needed a home or care? How about your partner's parent or relative?

❖ Is there a history of substance or alcohol abuse in your family or extended family?

❖ To what extent do your family's opinions affect your behavior and decisions?

❖ In general, do you see your family relationships as healthy? Now versus when you were a child?

❖ Does (or did) your family keep secrets? Are there any you're still holding from your childhood?

QUESTIONS TO EXPLORE AS A COUPLE

❖ Do you or your partner treat each other differently around family?

❖ Do you or your partner act differently around family?

❖ How involved are your families in your relationship?

❖ Are your families supportive of the relationship? If not, why? Are they right?

❖ How do your families get along? Are there many occasions when they are all in the same place at the same time?

❖ If you are a racially mixed couple, how does your family or society treat you when you go out? Does that affect your relationship?

Observations of Your Partner

❖ How does your partner treat their parents? Other family members?

❖ Does your partner get along with their family? Is their experience of family a positive one?

Self-Observations

❖ How does your relationship with your partner affect the quality of your relationship with your family?

❖ How does your relationship with your family affect the quality of your relationship with your partner?

❖ How do you feel about your partner's family? Do you get along? Are you comfortable with your partner's family?

❖ How do your partner's parents treat you?

❖ Does your family like and get along with your partner?

❖ How do your parents treat your partner?

❖ How do you feel about your partner visiting their family? With you? Without you?

❖ Are you willing to go to family outings without your partner?

❖ Does your partner's cultural background matter to you? Does it matter to your families?

CHAPTER SIXTEEN

Friends

e have a gay friend, Robert, who deeply values privacy. He would ideally prefer to have his partner, Jerry, be his constant companion and vice versa. Robert's preference would be to keep socializing outside of their union to a minimum. Jerry, on the other hand, has numerous friends and often chooses to spend time with them by going to parties, camping, and inviting them over for meals. This is a case where one or both partners will need to compromise or change in order for them to be together, and it may simply not be negotiable.

Friends can be your greatest blessing or your biggest problem. Take a careful look at who your friends are, who your partner's friends are, and how much of an influence they are in your life and relationship. If your partner has a best friend whom you don't get along with, problems are bound to arise. If you have friends who always meddle in your business, that can mean trouble, too. On the other hand, friends can have a lot of impact in a positive way, too. They can offer support and companionship and add variety to daily routines. Friends can also be a sounding board, offering a helpful perspective in times of need.

Consider the age-old saying "Birds of a feather flock together." If you don't feel comfortable around your partner's friends, take another look at your partner. There is usually a reason that they are friends. If you find your partner's friends to be trustworthy and nourishing, allow that to reflect on your partner as well. Keep in mind that we often tend to take on the characteristics of those with whom we closely associate. Early in the relationship, it is wise to also consider how much time each of you feels it is necessary to spend with friends, either in person or on the phone.

You may even want to ask your partner's friends about your partner, as they may have some helpful hints. When we first met, I asked one of Steven's female friends if he was as "good as he seemed." I respected her and felt she would tell me if there was something major I should know and had overlooked. By the same token, if your partner doesn't have any friends, consider why that's so.

QUESTIONS TO ASK EACH PARTNER

❖ How important are friendships to you?

❖ What do you consider the qualities of a good friend?

❖ Do you have a few close friends or a wide circle of acquaintances?

❖ Are most of your current friends childhood pals, work buddies, neighbors, etc.?

❖ Do you see yourself as an extrovert or introvert?

❖ Do you generally follow through on commitments to friends?

❖ Are you like your friends? Do you want to be?

❖ How subject to peer pressure are you?

❖ In general, are your friends a good influence on you?

❖ How much weight do you give to your friends' opinions?

❖ Upon what activities are your friendships based (work, gossip, sports, shopping, eating, drinking, flirting, etc.)?

❖ How much time do you need to spend alone with your friends (and without your partner)?

❖ How do you feel about your partner going out with friends (without you)?

❖ Are your partner's friends trustworthy?

❖ Are your friends primarily single? Married? How does this affect your relationship?

❖ What role do friends of the opposite sex (or same sexual orientation) play in your life and relationship?

❖ How do you feel about your partner having friends of the opposite sex (or same sexual orientation)?

❖ What role do your old loves or ex-spouses play in your present life? What is the quality of your current relationships with past partners? Do you get along?

❖ Are there any old friends/partners that you feel still involved with or with whom you feel unfinished?

❖ If your partner was uncomfortable with the quality or quantity of time you spend with your friends (of either sex), would you be willing to make changes?

❖ How do you feel about friends showing up unexpectedly? Do you feel strongly that friends should call before coming over?

❖ How do you feel about overnight guests?

❖ How does your relationship affect the quality of your friendships?

❖ Do you go to a certain friend to talk over problems or seek advice?

❖ Do you have a friend with whom you share the intimate details of your relationship?

❖ How much privacy around your life and problems do you prefer?

❖ Have you ever lost a friend over something you did? If so, explain.

❖ Are you good at keeping in touch with old friends?

❖ How easy is it for you to meet new friends? How/where do you usually meet people?

❖ Is there anyone in your life whom you consider a mentor?

QUESTIONS TO EXPLORE AS A COUPLE

❖ How much time do you spend as a couple with friends?

❖ Are your and your partner's friends supportive of your relationship? Does their opinion matter to you?

❖ Do your and your partner's friends encourage monogamy?

❖ Do your friends and your partner's friends get along?
Do you feel comfortable inviting them all to the same gatherings?

❖ Do you both think your partner should be consulted before friends are invited over, out with the two of you, or over for dinner (when the partner is directly involved)?

OBSERVATIONS OF YOUR PARTNER

❖ Is your partner a good friend to you? To others?

❖ Do you see your partner as an introvert or an extrovert? How does this affect you?

❖ Is your partner supportive of your friendships?

❖ Does your partner act differently or treat you differently around friends?

SELF-OBSERVATIONS

❖ Do you respect your partner's friends?

❖ How do you feel about going out with your partner's friends or colleagues?

❖ Do you feel welcome in your partner's circle of friends? Do you have a sense of belonging?

❖ Are your partner's friends a good influence on you?

❖ Are you willing to adopt your partner's "culture" in terms of friends, their values, and lifestyles?

❖ Are you like your partner's friends? Do you want to be?

❖ Is there jealousy between you and your partner's friends?
   If so, how do you work it out?

❖ Do you feel your partner's friends are more important to your
   partner than you are? If so, how do you handle that feeling?

❖ Are your friends more important to you than your partner is?

❖ Do you feel comfortable introducing your partner to your friends?

❖ Do your friends like your partner?

❖ Have your friends also befriended your partner; do partners
   play a role in your circle of friends?

❖ How much of your time or conversation with friends is spent talking
   about your partner or relationship? Is it positive or negative talk?

❖ Do you and/or your partner have a best friend other than each other?
   If so, how do you all get along? Are you included in their friendship?
   Do you include your partner in your friendship with your best friend?

❖ Are there things you say or do with your friends that you wouldn't say
   or do with your partner? What/why?

✳

CHAPTER SEVENTEEN

Education and Intelligence

 fell in love with Steven underwater as he taught me to scuba dive. I distinctly remember watching him as he taught me the basic skills, surrounded by turquoise water and green sea turtles. In the magic of the moment, I was impressed with his knowledge, competence, and patience, and I especially loved that he could teach me something new and wonderful.

A high priority in finding a mate was finding someone I could learn from, and who was also willing to learn from me. When two people come together and enrich each other's lives and embrace an attitude of lifelong learning, they are able to keep the relationship vital. Even after years of knowing someone, if both partners are still learning and growing, the relationship need never become stagnant. More important than formal education is your compatibility in your willingness to continue learning.

Formal education may impact a relationship, however, if one partner is highly intellectual or educated and the other is not. Although formal education is not the only way to become educated, to some—and/or their families—it represents status and identity. Attitudes about these issues can affect relationships. Another issue arises if one or both partners has a desire to continue their education but can only do so within the relationship if their partner is supportive. Unfulfilled goals, or a lack of support, often lead to problems.

Questions related to education and the raising of children are found in the chapter on "Children." Questions related to goals can be found in the "Future" chapter.

QUESTIONS TO ASK EACH PARTNER

❖ Where did you go to school?

❖ How much formal education do you have?

❖ Did you go to college? If so, what were your experiences? Did you live in the dorms or in an apartment? What did you study in college?

❖ Did you like school? Did you do well?

❖ Did you get in trouble? If so, for what offenses?

❖ Which extracurricular activities did you participate in?
Did you belong to a particular group at school (the athletes, the party animals, the cheerleaders, etc.)?

❖ What are you well trained in or qualified to do?

❖ What experiences have been your greatest source of learning?

❖ Do you want to continue your education (formally or informally)? How? What do you want to learn more about?

❖ How do you feel about education? How highly do you value education?

❖ What are your beliefs about adult education (e.g., life-long importance, valuable, waste of money, not for me, too time-consuming, etc.)?

❖ Did you go, or are you planning to go, to your high school reunions? How do you feel about taking your partner with you? How do you feel about going to your partner's reunions?

❖ How do you define intelligence?

❖ How important is intelligence to you in choosing a partner?

❖ How intelligent do you feel you are?

❖ In what ways do you seek out intellectual growth?

❖ What do you see as the difference between intelligence and wisdom?

❖ Do you consider yourself wise? Do you respect your life decisions?

QUESTIONS TO EXPLORE AS A COUPLE

❖ Can you/do you teach each other things? Is it okay for one of you to be better at something or know something the other doesn't?

❖ Can the two of you carry on mutually stimulating conversations based on your intelligence or education levels, or is there an imbalance that makes communication and understanding difficult? If so, does this matter to you?

❖ Will differences or similarities in your education levels create a challenge in the relationship? (For example, if you are both highly educated, will one have to give up their career or lower their career ambitions in order to raise a family? Is there academic or career competition between you? If one of you is formally educated and the other is not, will your families be judgmental about the differences between you?)

Observations of Your Partner

❖ Do you respect your partner's intelligence?

❖ Do you consider your partner wise? Do you respect their life decisions?

❖ Does your partner respect your intelligence and education (formal or informal)?

Self-Observations

❖ Do you have any prejudices or beliefs around your education or your partner's education (e.g., where they went to school, whether they had more or less education than you, how long it took to complete, etc.)?

❖ Do you think your partner's level of education will be an issue with your family?

❖ Are you willing to support your partner in continuing their education (by helping out around the house more or providing financial or emotional support, encouragement, etc.)?

 List the things you are an "expert" on or are well versed in that you could share with or teach your partner. What are your talents and areas of interest? From your observations of your partner, what would you like to learn from them?

PART FOUR

Where Are You Going?

MONEY

WORK

FUTURE

CHAPTER EIGHTEEN

Money

efore Steven and I met, he went to a party with a male friend. When they arrived, they discovered that this "party" was actually a gathering for singles. At first they thought it would be an excellent place to meet women. However, they were quickly turned off when, by way of introduction, the first questions out of the women's mouths were, "What do you do, and how much money do you make?" Steven and his friend felt that questions about their income within the first few moments of meeting were in as bad taste as asking the women, as a criterion for a date, "How soon can we have sex?"

Money may well be one of the biggest issues in a relationship, and it is also an extremely sensitive subject. Besides the obvious in terms of purchasing ability, money is also wrapped up with issues of self-concept, power, greed, honesty, trust, safety, freedom, and lifestyle. Use care in how you approach this subject. No one wants to feel they are being used (or chosen as a partner) because of their money. In the early stages of a relationship, or before one begins, familiarize yourself with these questions, and consider what you have to offer and what you want in this arena. Then, simply observe the situation until you are familiar enough with your partner to discuss these issues. These questions will need to be addressed directly when you are considering a more serious commitment.

One question that is reasonable to address early on is, "What are your feelings about who should pay when you go out?" As a woman, I always handled this situation by offering my share of the money spent until it was clear how the man felt about it. However, some men are offended when their date offers money and some are offended when their date doesn't. Talking about it directly or saying, "If you buy this time, I'll buy the next," is one way of handling the situation in these changing times.

Keep in mind that money issues can change over time. What you see now may not be what you get down the line. Consider the vow "For richer for poorer" carefully before you say, "I do." One woman, Denise, lamented that when she and her husband were married, money was always an issue, and it put stress on the marriage that, in part, eventually led to their divorce. After he remarried, she watched enviously as his new wife enjoyed all the benefits of the wealth he had acquired over time. Money can come and money can go, so more important than how much someone makes is their attitude about money, the way that they manage it, their responsibility toward debt, their generosity, and how they handle the stress that not having it—and having it—can create.

Money management can be handled very differently too. One married couple may prefer to keep their accounts separate and share expenses, while others merge all their money into joint accounts. There isn't a right or wrong way to do it as long as you talk about it and agree.

David and Lia encountered challenges adjusting to married life because Lia had been raised not to use credit cards unless she could pay off the entire amount by the time the bill came. Hence, she only bought things that she could afford. David, on the other hand, believed that "he who dies with the most debt wins." His belief was that you only live once, so as long as you are able to pay your monthly minimum payment, you should buy whatever you want. Their two styles were in direct opposition. This situation can be pretty scary—particularly when you suddenly realize that by saying, "I do," you take on financial responsibility for your spouse's actions as well.

Another couple was on the verge of getting engaged when they received a copy of *Intellectual Foreplay* and began discussing the questions. When they got to this section, they began to discover their incompatibilities. She felt prenuptial agreements were a good idea. She had been a successful actress since she was a child and had made a considerable amount of money prior to their relationship. He, on the other hand, felt prenuptial agreements were a statement of lack of faith in the relationship—the "out" clause. While this wasn't the only issue on which they disagreed, it was a major catalyst in their break-up. Had they stopped to self-observe, she would have realized that she had trust issues with him regarding money, and he would have realized that he had fear of abandonment issues with her, both hidden under the issue of prenuptial agreements. The "event" of their disagreement wasn't as much the issue as their inability to find responses to each other that were accepting and that created mutually satisfying outcomes.

QUESTIONS TO ASK EACH PARTNER

❖ What are your attitudes about money? Do you feel a sense of scarcity or abundance when you think about money?

❖ What are your financial goals?

❖ Are you comfortable financially with the amount you currently make?

❖ How much stress do money issues cause in your life?

❖ What is the earning potential in your present career?

❖ Do you feel competent managing money?

❖ What do you do with your money? Spend? Save? Invest? Gamble?

❖ What do you spend money on? What are your priorities?

❖ How good are you at saving for major expenses?

❖ Do you consider yourself frugal, impulsive, cheap, a big spender?

❖ Do you need a savings account to be comfortable or happy? If so, how much money needs to be in the account for you to feel comfortable?

❖ Do you go shopping as entertainment or as a necessity?

❖ How much time do you spend shopping for nonessential items (fancy clothes or shoes, electronics, toys, jewelry, etc.)?

❖ How much money do you spend on clothes? Massages? Hair? Nails?

❖ Do you like to shop at garage sales and flea markets? If so, how often, and approximately how much do you spend?

❖ Do you have any outstanding debts? If so, how much?

❖ Are your taxes up to date? What are your beliefs and practices around taxes? Do you hire someone to do them? Do you do them yourself?

❖ Do you have good credit?

❖ What are your beliefs and practices around using credit?

❖ Do you trust yourself with a credit card?

❖ What are your feelings about bankruptcy? Have you ever been bankrupt?

❖ Would you ever consider claiming bankruptcy?

❖ Do you tend to pay your bills on time? Are you able to pay them?

❖ What are your monthly expenses?

❖ Do you pay child support or alimony?

❖ What do you need to buy to be happy? Do you need a new vehicle each year, a trip overseas, new clothes each month?

❖ How much money do you need to support your lifestyle? Are you able to make that much?

❖ How would you handle a forced change in lifestyle (due to a job loss or budgeting requirements while saving for a major purchase)?

❖ How do you feel about loaning money to family and/or friends?

❖ How do you feel about borrowing from family and friends?

❖ What are your feelings on prenuptial agreements (regarding debts and/or assets)? Would you be willing to sign one?

❖ What are your beliefs about men's and women's roles in terms of making money, supporting a family, etc.?

❖ How do you feel about supporting your partner? While they pursue an education or career change? While they are fighting an illness? While they manage the household or raise children? Indefinitely?

❖ Are you willing or able to support a partner or family?

❖ How do you feel about being supported by your partner?

❖ If your income greatly increased (either suddenly or gradually), what kind of lifestyle would you want to have? How would it change your relationships?

❖ If you won a sweepstakes or received an inheritance, would you still want to work? What would you do? How would it change your relationships?

❖ How are you planning for retirement?

❖ Do you play the stock market? To what extent?

❖ Do you gamble? If so, how often? How much money do you generally gamble?

❖ Has gambling ever affected your life in a negative way? A positive way?

❖ Have you ever been "used" for money?

❖ Have you ever "used" someone for money?

❖ Have you ever gotten involved or stayed involved with someone because of money?

QUESTIONS TO EXPLORE AS A COUPLE

❖ What are your feelings about who should pay when you go out? Who usually does? Are you okay with it?

❖ Do you each take financial responsibility for yourselves? Are you both able to take care of yourselves financially?

❖ Does it matter who makes more money?

❖ If you're living together (or planning to), who's in charge of the money?

❖ Do you combine accounts or keep separate ones?

❖ How do you divide the expenses? Food expenses? Household bills?

❖ How do you budget and prioritize expenses?

❖ Who does the "book work" or pays the bills?

❖ Who makes decisions about major expenses or purchases?

❖ If you moved in together, would both partners have to work in order to pay the bills?

❖ If you were to split up, do you foresee any problems around dividing up money/assets?

❖ Do both people know where all the important papers are kept and how to handle the bills if something happens to one partner?

❖ If one of you were to die, would the other be able to take over, knowing what needs to be done? Are you willing to discuss what needs to be done in terms of insurance, wills, trust funds, etc.?

OBSERVATIONS OF YOUR PARTNER

❖ Does your partner appear to be in control of their financial situation?

❖ Is your partner able to support himself/herself?

❖ How does your partner's financial potential look?

❖ Do you trust your partner with a credit card?

❖ Do you trust your partner with money-making/spending decisions?

❖ Do you trust your partner with your money?

❖ How do you feel about your partner gambling?

SELF-OBSERVATIONS

❖ How important is money in your choice of a partner? Is it important that they be prosperous or match your own income level?

❖ If your partner suddenly had little or no money, would you still be interested in them? If you suddenly had no money, would your partner still be interested in you?

※

CHAPTER NINETEEN

Work

I used to date a man who owned his own retail business, and he could never completely relax when we went on vacations. He would have to call in regularly, and everywhere we went he insisted on going into all the retail stores of the same type as his to "check out the competition." While his needs were certainly understandable, it is difficult when you can never get away from work or the telephone. Now, I have more empathy as Steven and I run three businesses in addition to our full-time jobs.

Dating someone who works for himself or herself is very different than dating someone who works for somebody else. While entrepreneurs are often confident and focused, they are also likely to have lots of time constraints and high stress levels over keeping everything running smoothly and hiring and firing employees. This kind of workload requires plenty of communication and understanding in other areas of the relationship, such as time and housecleaning.

Work is often an area of our partners' lives that we don't know much about. Often, they drive away in the morning and we don't know what their lives are like until they return home again. Yet a person's identity can be wrapped up in what they do for a living. Their business also affects their stress level, amount of free time, income level, sense of competence, and general sense of happiness. Responsibility, ethics, environmental concerns, and many other value structures are evident in what a person chooses as a career, so discussing these questions with a partner can often give you much valuable information about who they are.

Another thing to consider is that what someone does for a living and how much they make can always change. Finding a partner who is supportive of you and your goals is as important as finding one who is supportive of what you are currently doing. One man we spoke with, Vern, was admittedly driven to succeed, but when asked if he felt he was successful, he seemed perplexed—as if success is something you *strive* for, not something that is *achievable*. The challenge is that there are always higher levels of success, so if you don't define what success means to you, you may never realize it when you get there.

While the questions in this chapter don't emphasize the intense workload that a homemaker has, it is acknowledged that taking care of a home and raising a family is also "work." If one of you is a homemaker, explore these questions in light of that being your current career, and discuss how you feel about it.

It is interesting to note that people have written to let us know how useful *Intellectual Foreplay* was in helping them choose business partners and develop relationships with team members on their jobs. While certain questions and categories are obviously not appropriate to discuss with potential business partners, others will serve the purpose nicely.

More questions related to life goals and dreams—which may be related to work—can be found in the "Future" chapter.

QUESTIONS TO ASK EACH PARTNER

❖ What do you do, specifically, for work? Are you self-employed?

❖ Are you a homemaker? If so, do you want to re-enter the work force? What did you do before homemaking? What would you like to do again?

❖ How did you choose your current career?

❖ How time-consuming is your work? How many hours per week do you put in?

❖ Are you happy with your job?

❖ Is your job a career for you or just a way to make money?

❖ How committed are you to your profession?

❖ Is your job in alignment with your values?
  If not, are you attempting to change your job?

❖ Do you consider yourself a "workaholic"?

❖ How stressful is your job?

❖ What's a typical day on the job like for you?

❖ What kind of status do you give your job?
  Are you proud of what you do?

❖ What does "success" mean to you?

❖ Do you consider yourself successful?

❖ Do you work alone, or do you rely on teamwork?

❖ Do you like your boss or the people whom you work with?

❖ Do you look forward to going to work each day, accept it, or dread it?

❖ Do you consider yourself ambitious/goal-oriented in your business, or are you content with your job as it is now?

❖ Do you intend to stay in the same line of work? If not, what kind of changes are you expecting or planning? Is there some kind of work that you would rather do?

❖ If you could do absolutely anything and get paid for it, what would you want to do?

❖ What are your goals around your job, and how do you plan to achieve them?

❖ Would you be willing to relocate for business? Under what circumstances?

❖ Would you be willing to relocate for your partner's business?

❖ Do you give your all to your job or just do what you need to do to get the job done?

❖ Does your job require home work?

❖ Do you have an office in your home?

❖ How organized are you? Are you good at paperwork and filing?

❖ Are you able to let go of your job when you are at home?

❖ Do you have to be "on call" or work weekends and evenings?

❖ Does your work have upward mobility potential? Are you expecting promotions?

❖ Does your work require a lot of travel?

❖ Do you have to socialize with or entertain business associates? How often? How elaborate do such events need to be?

❖ How do you feel about being asked about work at the end of the day?

❖ Which has a higher priority for you, work or relationships?

❖ Is it okay for your partner to call you at work?

❖ Is it okay for your partner to visit you at work? Go to work with you?

❖ How does your relationship affect the quality of your work?

❖ How does your work affect the quality of your relationship?

❖ How do you feel about combining business and friendships? Business and family?

❖ How do you feel about going into business with or working with your partner?

❖ Is there anyone you consider a mentor in your line of business?

❖ Are you a mentor to anyone on the job?

❖ Do you consider yourself a good employee/worker/employer? How would you like to improve?

❖ What was the best job you ever had? What did you like about it, and which of your skills did it utilize? What was the worst?

❖ If you were to honestly write yourself a letter of reference for a job, what would you say?

❖ If you lost the job you are trained to do and had a hard time finding another one, would you be willing to do any job just to make money while you were looking, even though it might not be a professional or career-oriented one?

❖ If you were out of work, to what lengths would you go to get a new job?

❖ Have you ever been unemployed for long periods of time? If so, what happened?

❖ At what age do you expect to retire?

❖ Does your work, or do you, have a retirement plan?

QUESTIONS TO EXPLORE AS A COUPLE

❖ If you have children, how will you balance work and family? Will one of you stay home? If so, which one?

❖ Is there competition between you in the realm of work? If so, how does it affect the relationship?

OBSERVATIONS OF YOUR PARTNER

❖ How does your partner respond when you ask about their work?

❖ Does your partner talk positively about their work, or do they sound unhappy and complaining? Does this vary or is it a constant attitude?

❖ How does your partner respond when you talk about your work?

❖ Does your partner support you in your work?

❖ Does your partner appear to have a balance in their life between hours spent on business activities and other activities?

SELF-OBSERVATIONS

❖ How do you feel about your partner's work? Do you respect what they do? How supportive are you of your partner's work/business?

❖ Have you ever seen your partner in a professional role?

❖ How do you feel about your partner's time commitment to business?

❖ How do you feel when your partner travels on business?

❖ Do you call your partner when you're away on business? If so, how often?

❖ If your partner travels, how often do you want or expect to hear from them?

❖ How do you feel about dating people you work with?

CHAPTER TWENTY

Future

n my "hippie days," I bought an old blue school bus that I wanted to turn into a mobile home and drive across the country. While there was nothing wrong with a vision like this, finding a partner who shared the same dream could have been challenging—to say the least. Although Steven had no interest in living in a school bus, he used to dream about sailing around the world. While our outward goals were different, the underlying values were the same: travel, adventure, and meeting new people. While I no longer want to live in a bus, those values are still with me.

When you share your dreams with each other, look beneath the surface to discover the values that are likely to be carried into the future of your relationship, and see if you can create common dreams that include these values. Exploring your vision of the future is as valuable, if not more valuable, as reviewing past events. After all, the future is what you have to share. Whether or not your goals are in alignment can be a determining factor in making the "right choice." Even if everything else is a match, if one person plans to travel the globe like a nomad while the other wants a home with a white-picket fence, it isn't going to work—at least not easily.

How do you envision your future? Write down a description of your goals for each of the areas listed below. Write them in present tense, as if they are already true, and be specific! Allow this to be a template for what you want to create. For example: "My home sits on a hillside with an incredible view of the ocean off Maui. I love to watch the sunsets from the deck, etc."

How do you see yourself in ten years? What will these things be like:

- Your home
- Your health
- Your work
- Your accomplishments
- Your relationship
- Your lifestyle
- Your spiritual life
- Your hobbies/activities
- Your family
- Your friends

Share your visions with each other and refer to them often. Pay attention to whether your visions are compatible.

Evaluate your own commitment to your goals. In terms of priorities, which would come first: your relationship or the manifestation of your dreams? Bob and Karen realized several years into their relationship that his dream of bicycling around the world was becoming more and more important to him, while she didn't have any desire to participate. It appeared that in order for them to stay together, he was going to have to give up his dream. The older Bob got, the less willing he was to let life pass by without going for it. Rather than breaking up, they decided he would take his expedition with other people and she would fly to meet him in different parts of the world. Sometimes it is necessary to get creative with your solutions, and sometimes you may opt to let your relationship go in order to live out your passions.

One of the realities of "happily-ever-after" or "'til death do us part" that we overlook when we are young is that this means we are going to grow old together. Aging has a whole set of circumstances that go with it that need to be considered, not the least of which is the fulfillment of our life purpose. Some major life changes take place when the kids move out (if you have children) and when one or both of you retires. The "Appearance and Attraction," "Health," "Religion and Spirituality," "Work," "Family," "Children," and "Money" chapters touch on some of the practical issues that will arise through the years.

Retirement is an exciting and challenging time in a relationship that requires some conscious re-negotiation of roles, use of time, and use of space. My parents, who have been married for half a century, say that retirement has been the most romantic time of their relationship. They are now able to provide each other the kind of companionship that wasn't possible when work and children pulled them in different directions. There is also a sense of safety that comes with sharing so many years and challenges together. They inspire the entire neighborhood as they take their daily walks together, holding hands and talking.

There are specific issues that come with retirement that aren't immediately obvious and which require communication. (Please pardon the gender biases in the following scenario, and change them to match your situation, if necessary.) At the time of retirement, jobs *outside* the home stop, but the jobs *inside* the home continue. In a situation where the wife has taken care of the house and kids while the husband worked (or while they both worked), there is a marked opportunity for him to retire and pursue other interests; however, it is important to recognize that she may like to retire as well. Thus a re-negotiation of jobs, such as preparing meals and cleaning, is necessary. Sharing responsibilities that used to be entirely "the other person's job" is not always easy.

It is also a major shift in the relationship if one partner used to be home alone all the time and then suddenly has a constant companion. By the same token, the one who used to have their days filled with work suddenly has time to fill and a partner's needs to handle. In this same scenario, he may feel like the household is not his, as it has been her domain all these years. In his eyes, he may feel like an alien, and to her, he may be an invader. Re-negotiating the division and sharing of household space becomes necessary.

One woman said that since her husband was ten years older, she was nowhere near ready to retire when he did. His sudden availability and her lack of time created dynamics that they had to navigate to keep their relationship healthy. Role reversals, such as the man being at home while the woman works, can also be a challenge to overcome.

Issues of self-worth can also come to the surface when one's job provided a sense of purpose that has suddenly ended. If both partners are going through this change in their life roles at the same time, it can be a double whammy to the relationship. Communication is very important in ironing out these possible challenges.

Once you get beyond the decisions and the rebuilding, retirement is an awesome opportunity for pursuing passions that you weren't able to during your working years. The key is to retire your job, *not* your body or your mind. As pointed out in the "Education and Intelligence" chapter, adopting a style of lifelong learning through reading and taking classes will help. Then you can share your newly discovered interests and activities with each other.

In detail, describe what you want to be like when you are old. Where do you want to live? How will you spend your time? How will people think of you? How will you feel about the life you've led? What will the quality of your relationships be?

Questions to Ask Each Partner

❖ What are your goals? Dreams? In which ways do you live in alignment with them?

❖ How important are your goals to you? To what lengths would you go to realize them?

❖ Is there anything that you're hoping to do someday?

❖ Is there anything that you really want to learn how to do or know more about?

❖ Is there anything you feel you must accomplish before you die?

❖ What steps do you need to take to achieve these goals?

❖ How do you feel about self-exploration, personal growth, discovery, and change?

❖ How do you handle change? New ideas?

❖ How willing to change are you? To what extent do you want your life to change?

❖ How do you envision your lifestyle in old age?

❖ At what age do you believe "old age" begins?

❖ At what age do you expect or plan to retire?

❖ What do you intend to do during your retirement years?

❖ If you were to die today, would you be satisfied with the way you've lived?

❖ If you could have one wish, what would it be?

QUESTIONS TO EXPLORE AS A COUPLE

❖ Are your goals and dreams compatible?

❖ How do you envision your relationship in old age?

❖ Can you picture growing old and enjoying time together?

❖ How do you want to spend your "golden years"? What activities do you anticipate wanting to explore after you retire?

❖ How are you preparing for the change in needs that growing old brings with it?

❖ If one person is older than the other and reaches retirement age first, how will you handle the change in roles? Will the younger of the two be expected to retire at the same time? Would they want to?

❖ When retirement approaches, how do you envision re-negotiating roles, responsibilities, and use of space within the house?

❖ Have you maintained (or will you maintain) a support network of family and friends to assist you as you grow older?

Self-Observations

❖ Do you respect your partner's goals and visions?

❖ How supportive of your partner's dreams are you? How supportive of your dreams are they?

❖ When you imagine growing old with your partner, or spending the rest of your life with them, how do you feel?

✳

PART FIVE

Can We Live Together?

HOME

HOUSEHOLD RESPONSIBILITIES
AND HABITS

FOOD AND COOKING

BATHROOM

PETS

VEHICLES

PLANTS AND GARDEN

CHAPTER TWENTY ONE

Home

hen I moved in with Steven, his home was a bit of a bachelor pad. Recently, after years of living together, buying a home, and collecting treasures, he commented about how every year our home looks more and more like my parents' home. I have always loved the kind of things my parents filled their home with and the atmosphere there. Hence, I unconsciously transformed our home into a similar environment.

If a person's home is their castle, you can be sure they also have strong feelings about what they want and don't want in that castle. The environment they were raised in will influence their expectations and desires, too. Where you *want* to live, where you are *willing* to live, and where you will *have* to live can also have a strong influence on your happiness and comfort and, consequently, the relationship. Wendee and her partner are in the midst of a long-term, committed relationship, but they both prefer to live in their own homes. Where your partner wants to live may not be a negotiable item, so explore it carefully.

A pregnant woman recently bought *Intellectual Foreplay* and explored the questions with her fiancé (perhaps just a little too late...). When discussing where they would both like to live, she discovered that he wanted to stay in the mountains, while her ideal was to move close to the beach. Under the circumstances, they will likely compromise; however, it pays to discover these types of differences early in the dating stages.

Preferences in this area can change with circumstances. Family responsibilities change housing needs as children are born or move out, and aging parents can also affect your choices over time. Another consideration that frequently comes up in relationships is jobs that require mobility. One woman and her husband had moved twenty-three times in twenty-eight years of marriage due to his work!

QUESTIONS TO ASK EACH PARTNER

❖ What does the concept of "home" mean to you?

❖ Is there a place that you consider to be "home"—regardless of where you live?

❖ Describe the home(s) you were raised in.

❖ Describe your dream house.

❖ Do you presently own a home? Would you rather own or rent, or does it matter to you?

❖ What are your expectations for a house? How big do you want it to be?

❖ Do you have dreams of building or designing your own home?

❖ What amenities do you expect? What are your needs in terms of number of bedrooms, office, studio, yard, etc.?

❖ What features are mandatory for you in a home (storage space, kitchen counters, etc.)?

❖ What are you willing to settle for in a home?

❖ Where do you want to live (city, country, mountains, beach, specific states, etc.)?

❖ Do you like warm or cool temperatures and climates?

❖ How do you feel about living in a condo, apartment, tent, mobile home (or school bus!), etc.?

❖ What are your preferences around decorating styles and colors?

❖ Do you like antique, new, used, or modern furniture, etc.?

❖ Do you like each room to have a different theme or to create one theme throughout the house, or whatever, wherever?

❖ Is decorating a shared task or one person's responsibility? Whose?

❖ Is it okay for your partner to move furniture or redecorate without consulting you?

❖ Do you allow guests to smoke in the house?

❖ How much privacy do you need in your home?

❖ Do you have your own room? Do you need a space that's exclusively yours, or are you comfortable sharing the whole house as common space?

❖ Do you have a favorite room in the house?

QUESTIONS TO EXPLORE AS A COUPLE

❖ If you move in together, will you find a new home, or will one of you move in with the other?

❖ Will your possessions combine easily?

❖ If you move in together, will you have housemates?
If you already live together, would you consider getting housemates?

❖ Are your tastes in furniture and decor similar/compatible?
Does your home, or will your home, reflect both partners' tastes?
Whose furniture will you use?

OBSERVATIONS OF YOUR PARTNER

❖ What does the environment in your partner's home communicate
to you about their values and interests?

❖ Does your partner treat you as a guest in their home or as though
you live there? Which do you prefer?

SELF-OBSERVATIONS

❖ Do you feel comfortable in your partner's home?

❖ Do you feel welcomed when you visit?

❖ If your partner has roommates, do you feel welcomed by them?
Do you get along with them?

❖ Do you like your partner's household items/decor?

❖ If you are moving into your partner's home, how comfortable do you
anticipate feeling there? Is your partner making room for your things?

❖ If your partner is moving into your home, how hard will it be for you
to share your space? Are you willing to make room for your partner's
belongings in your home?

✳

CHAPTER TWENTY TWO

Household Responsibilities and Habits

an and Thomas faced an interesting challenge when she first spent the night with him. She discovered that he liked to keep the stereo or television on all night long. She had grown up in a household that was quiet and peaceful and valued silence—especially at night. Thomas had lived alone for a long time and liked having background noise twenty-four hours a day. While neither was right or wrong, this was a non-negotiable item for Jan, as she couldn't sleep with the noise. They chose to discuss their differences and accept each other's needs. Thomas decided he would be willing to transform his need for noise into an appreciation of silence at night in honor of keeping the relationship.

When we asked people what one should know before getting seriously involved, numerous questions were brought up around household issues and personal habits. One woman chose to leave her partner, in part, because she felt a home should feel "lived in," while he felt everything should always be in place to the extent that he kept the spices alphabetized in the kitchen. This kind of incompatibility could leave both partners total-ly frustrated. Knowing your partner's preferences, working out agreements in advance, and having a shared level of tolerance for clutter is helpful.

Simply accepting that one partner may seldom if ever do certain chores, but will responsibly do others, can also help. It's been known as "division of labor" throughout the ages, and as long as it is equitable and mutually agreed upon, it can be a viable solution to household compatibility. After forty-five years of marriage, Peggy looked through *Intellectual Foreplay* and realized that she was the only one in her family who cleaned toilets. She multiplied three bathrooms by fifty-two weeks a year by forty-five years and realized that she had cleaned 7,020 toilets during the course of her marriage—so far! However, she had never mowed a lawn or changed the oil in the car, nor had she had to work outside of the home while she raised kids. While cleaning toilets was not her preference, it was a tradeoff she was willing to make when she looked at the total picture. When you compare what each partner does, be sure to look at the big picture rather than just an individual chore.

A person's habits, lifestyle, and household routine aren't a problem when they live alone, but when a partner moves in, one's way of being suddenly impacts the other. After extended periods of time living alone and not having to consider anyone else, it's easy to get "spoiled." The little things that become overwhelmingly annoying, threatening the relationship, are often signs of bigger issues. For example, little habits might reveal a lack of consideration for the other person, lack of respect for the other person's needs, lack of self-respect, hygiene problems, or lack of thinking as a couple. Pay attention when the little things get to you, and look behind them to see what else is there. By the same token, don't assume that a few bad habits necessarily point to serious, relationship-destroying problems. Control-and-approval battles often cause an inability to see solutions and compromises. When we let go of resistance to our partners, resourceful solutions will often reveal themselves.

When Steven and I moved in together, we found that our body temperature gauges are exactly the opposite. He is hot at night when we go to bed, seldom wanting covers, while I am usually cold at this time, pulling the covers up. In the morning, however, my body temperature is so hot I can't stand the covers and Steven is then cold. Neither of us is right or wrong in how our metabolism works; however, it is necessary to resist the urge to say, "My way is right." Instead, being clear and accepting about our differences allows us to find solutions that work for us. Now, we simply laugh about it and just take turns pulling up the covers or throwing them off.

Some of the questions in this category may draw your attention to things that you should be aware of but that don't necessarily affect you one way or the other. One person may need eight hours' sleep, while the other needs only six. As long as you are each willing to respect what the other needs, there shouldn't be a problem. Difficulty comes when one partner tries to make the other partner do it "their way" on non-negotiable items.

Sylvia and Max have a challenge in that she wakes up and immediately feels talkative and cheerful. Her brain is fully engaged upon the first ring of the alarm, and she wants to discuss the problems of the world, find solutions, and plan out the day. Max, on the other hand, wakes up slowly. He sets the alarm half an hour before he really has to get up, allowing it to ring every five minutes and wake him up slowly. He has no interest in talking about anything when he first wakes up. This requires Max and Sylvia to acknowledge, accept, and honor their differences.

Since many habits can be changed, observe yourself—your habits and their importance to you—and look at the impact of them on your relationship. Ask yourself, "What's it like to live with me?" If you don't like the answer, make the necessary changes. Communicate about what you each prefer, let go of resistance, and consider your options. Be clear about those issues you are willing to compromise on and those which are not negotiable.

Many of these questions pertain to any roommate situation, so if you're searching for a housemate, explore this chapter—just be sure to skip the "sleeping together" questions! Virtually all the other chapters in this part of the book, "Can We Live Together?" will be useful for screening a roommate, too. Questions related to the financial responsibilities of sharing a household are found in the "Money" chapter.

QUESTIONS TO ASK EACH PARTNER

❖ What types of chores do you like and dislike?

❖ Are there any chores you refuse to do?

❖ Do you like to have a schedule for doing household chores, or do you prefer to just do things when time, need, and mood permit?

❖ Are you a clean person? Messy? Compulsive?

❖ How do you feel about hiring a house cleaner?

❖ Are you good at fixing things around the house?

❖ How is your tolerance for messes? Piles?

❖ Do you throw out junk mail as it comes in or pile it up?

❖ On a scale of one to ten, how clean do you expect your home to be?

❖ On a scale of one to ten, how organized are you?

❖ Do you keep things (old books, magazines, containers, etc.)?

❖ Do you consider yourself a pack rat?

❖ What kinds of things is it okay to throw away, give to charity, or sell at a garage sale?

❖ Do you put things back where they belong (in the place where you got them)?

❖ Do you close drawers and cabinets?

❖ Do you turn out lights as you leave a room?

❖ Do you lock the house? When you're home? At night? When you go out?

❖ Are you comfortable with the level of security in your home? Do you feel safe there?

❖ How many watts do you want your lightbulbs to be? Does your preference vary room to room?

❖ What are your views and practices in terms of recycling?

❖ Where do you put (or leave) your dirty laundry? Where do you put clothes that have been worn once or twice (the ones that aren't actually clean but still aren't too dirty)?

❖ Do you separate laundry by colors?

❖ Do you check the pockets before doing laundry?

❖ How do you feel about air conditioners?

❖ Do one of you have "ownership" of the garage? Do you have equal use of tools and work space?

❖ Do you like listening to music around the house? What kind? How loud?

❖ Do you have strong feelings about what is appropriate or inappropriate on your answering machine message (e.g., how much information should be on the tape, how often the message should be changed, whether names are included on the message, whose voice is on it, etc.)?

❖ Do you have a preference for types of messages (e.g., humorous, serious, etc.)?

❖ If you are living in the same home, does the answering machine message make it clear to the caller that there are two people at that number?

❖ How good are you about taking phone messages for other household members? Do you write messages down or just try to remember them? How responsible are you about passing them on?

❖ If there are critters in your house (mice, spiders, etc.), what do you do (try to catch them and put them out, kill them, trap them)?

❖ How do you feel about extermination and fumigation of the house? Yard?

❖ How often do change your sheets?

❖ How often do you feel the sheets should be changed?

❖ Do you make the bed each day? Do you care if the bed is made?

❖ How many hours of sleep do you require per night? Between which hours?

❖ Do you like to sleep snuggled together or on your own side of the bed?

❖ Do you like to sleep with the window open or closed? With a fan/heater on or off?

❖ Do you tend to get cold or hot at night? Do you like a lot of covers? Pajamas?

❖ Do you wear curlers, creams, or oils on your face or hair at night? Retainers or mouth guards?

❖ Are you a morning person or a night person?

❖ Do you wake up cheerful or grumpy? Quickly or slowly? Do you like to be left alone until you're fully awake or you've had coffee?

❖ Do you set the alarm for the time you need to get up or for an earlier time, pushing and re-pushing the snooze button (if so, how much earlier)?

❖ How do you feel about being awakened by your partner or phone calls during the night? Are you nice about it, or does it make you angry?

❖ Do you expect both partners to go to bed at the same time, or is it okay for one to stay up later? Would you get upset if this happened regularly? Do you expect both partners to get up at the same time?

❖ If you fell asleep on the couch at night, would you want to be awakened to go to bed or left there to sleep?

❖ Do you fall asleep with the television on at night?

❖ Do you read before you go to bed?

❖ How much time do you spend reading?
   Does this interfere with your relationships?

❖ Do you leave the light on at night?

❖ Do you leave the stereo on at night?

❖ Do you snore? Grind your teeth?

❖ Which habits of yours have been a challenge in relationships in the past? Which habits are likely to affect this relationship?

Questions to Explore as a Couple

❖ How do you divide up household chores? Are you comfortable with that division?

❖ As situations change, how flexible or negotiable are you about reassigning chores and duties (depending on who has time, who is going into town, etc.)?

❖ Do you tend to do whatever needs to be done regardless of whose "turn" it is, whose job it is, or how busy the other partner is?

❖ Whose job is it to bring in the mail from the box or home from the post office? Where do you put new mail?

❖ Who changes the lightbulbs?

❖ Who takes out the trash? Recycling?

❖ Who does the laundry? Do you each do your own laundry? Do you both do each other's laundry? Who does the household laundry (towels, sheets)?

❖ Who changes the sheets and makes the bed?

❖ Who is responsible for correspondence with family and friends? With the other person's family?

❖ Who makes business calls regarding doctor appointments, repairs, etc.?

OBSERVATIONS OF YOUR PARTNER

❖ Does your partner help with household chores?

❖ On a more basic note, does your partner do any of the following, and if so, does it bother you?

- Pop their knuckles?

- Pick their nose? (In front of others?)

- Bite their nails?

- Chew gum? (Often? sometimes? all the time?)

- Pick their ears with foreign objects?

- Belch or fart excessively or loudly, in public or private?

- Snore?

- "Pick" (constantly pick at acne or at their fingers)?

SELF-OBSERVATIONS

❖ Do you feel comfortable with the way your partner keeps their home?

❖ When you imagine sharing household responsibilities with your partner, how do you feel?

❖ Do you have any habits that would be challenging to live with? If so, are you willing to do anything about them?

✳

CHAPTER TWENTY THREE

Food
and Cooking

ne thing that I had to warn Steven about early in our relationship is that I have a hereditary need to eat when I'm hungry. If my blood sugar drops too low, I can turn into a raging monster. Since both of us are aware of this well in advance of any physically induced mood swing, we can take steps to avoid getting to that point—we always *keep food nearby!*

There are some who say the key to success in a relationship is compatibility in food preferences and habits. While it may not be the most important "ingredient," it can add ease to the relationship. In addition to metabolic needs, dietary differences can influence relationships. Vegetarians abound these days, in varying degrees of strictness. One will eat fish, but not fowl or red meat, while another won't eat any dairy products at all. Some refuse to have any meat products in their kitchens, while others don't mind preparing it for their families as long as they don't have to eat it. It's hard to keep track; some will eat only fruit, others only raw! Since these issues usually run deeper than mere preference—they're often based in core values, spirituality, and/or health requirements—it's necessary to discuss your eating habits to find out what is negotiable and what is not.

Who cooks and cleans is also something to explore. Tracy and Chris have resolved this issue by trading off. They've agreed that whoever cooks doesn't have to clean the kitchen. Both of them feel Chris is the better cook of the two, so he regularly puts the meals together while Tracy cleans up afterward.

For some, food and meals are symbolic of home and family, and there may be some very specific expectations. Sit-down meals at the table are important to some, while meals in front of the television are acceptable to others. One woman grew up in a large family, so throughout her whole childhood she had to fight for her share of the food. Consequently, she can't stand it when someone takes food off her plate. This is a simple issue to avoid, as long as a partner knows how you feel. Simply identify your own preferences first and then explore compatibility with your partner.

Alison was surprised to discover that her boyfriend, Dean, got completely agitated and grumpy any time they had to go to the grocery store together. The first time this happened, she didn't realize that the shopping itself was the problem, and she thought that she had done something wrong. It wasn't until she saw the pattern every time they went that she figured out that he just hated shopping. Once she understood the problem, she could help to solve it by going to the market alone. Had Dean done some self-observation, he would have become aware of what he was doing and been able to express his needs verbally rather than acting them out inappropriately.

After years of marriage, Steven and I had to laugh when he leaned over my shoulder as I was writing this and read out loud, "Who cleans the kitchen?" and I blurted out, "No one!"

QUESTIONS TO ASK EACH PARTNER

❖ What kinds of foods do you like?

❖ What kinds of foods don't you like?

❖ Is eating something you love to do, or is it just a necessity?

❖ Is there anything you won't or can't eat? Do you have any dietary restrictions?

❖ How often do you go on diets? How strict are the diets, and how strict are you?

❖ Are you a vegetarian? If so, how strict? Are you willing to have your partner eat meat at home? Are you willing to prepare or cook meat for your partner?

❖ Do you need each of the four food groups included in each meal?

❖ How much and how often do you eat? How many meals do you eat a day?

❖ Do you like/need to eat new and different things, or are you happy eating the "tried and true" recipes regularly?

❖ How do you feel about leftovers? Are you willing to eat the same thing a few days in a row?

❖ Do you feel insulted if everything on your partner's plate isn't eaten?

❖ Do you eat everything on your plate, always leave a few bites, or stop when you're full?

❖ Do you eat food off other people's plates? Do you mind if other people eat food off your plate?

❖ Do you snack between meals?

❖ Do you eat late at night?

❖ Do you cook? Do you like to cook?

❖ Do you consider yourself a good cook?

❖ Do you consider cooking an art or a necessary chore?

❖ Do you plan weekly menus or fix whatever you feel like at the time?

❖ Do you like to experiment with new recipes?

❖ How do you feel about cooking for company? Drop-in visitors?
Do you like to entertain?

❖ Do you make shopping lists or just buy whatever you feel like
at the time?

❖ How do you feel about eating while shopping in the grocery store
(sampling bulk items, eating things that you are about to buy, etc.)?

❖ Are you a coupon collector?

❖ What are your preferences or traditions around sit-down meals
(Sunday meals, dinner, every meal)?

❖ Where do you like to eat meals (in the dining room, in front of the
television, in bed, in the car, etc.)?

❖ Are there rooms in your home where eating is not allowed?

❖ Do you like to go out to eat? How often?

❖ Do you eat fast food?

❖ Do you tend to complain (regularly) about food or service
in restaurants?

❖ How long are you willing to wait in lines at restaurants?

❖ How do you feel about gratuities/tipping? Do you always tip 10%, 15%, 20% or tip according to service?

❖ How orderly do you expect the kitchen to be? How clean do you need the kitchen to be in order to feel comfortable?

❖ Do you have any personal rituals or schedules for cleaning the kitchen (for example, cleaning up before going to bed so it's clean in the morning)?

❖ Do you wash dishes after each meal or let them pile up?

❖ Do you put the dishes away? Do you put bowls with bowls, dishes with dishes, or put them wherever there is room?

❖ Do you, or how often do you, throw away old/moldy food in the refrigerator?

❖ Do you refill ice trays with water or put them back in the freezer empty or almost empty?

❖ Are you a coffee drinker? If so, how much? How often? How many cups do you need to get started in the morning?

❖ Do you feel that you have good table manners?

❖ Do you "double dip" your chips in public bowls of dip? Does it bother you if people double dip? (Double dip means to put the same chip back in the dip after you've already eaten part of the chip.)

QUESTIONS TO EXPLORE AS A COUPLE

❖ Do you like to cook meals together?

❖ Do you believe one or the other should always be responsible for cooking and cleaning? If so, who?

❖ Is it okay for each of you to create your own meals from time to time if you have different tastes or desires? How important is it to eat meals together?

❖ Are your food habits, likes, and dislikes compatible?

❖ Do one or the other of you have "ownership" of the kitchen?

❖ Who does the grocery shopping?

❖ When you go out to eat, who chooses the restaurant? Who pays? Is one person responsible for ordering for both people?

OBSERVATIONS OF YOUR PARTNER

❖ Does your partner have eating habits that bother you? Are you comfortable with your partner's table manners?

❖ Do your partner's table manners embarrass you when you eat in public?

❖ Does your partner lick their fingers, silverware, or plate when they eat? If so, does that bother or embarrass you?

❖ Does your partner chew with their mouth open?

❖ Do they talk with their mouth full?

❖ Do they chew loudly?

Self-Observations

❖ How important is it to you that your partner is a good cook?

❖ How important is it to you that your partner washes dishes?

❖ How do you feel when your partner complains about food or service in a restaurant?

❖ How do you handle it if your partner over- or under-tips?

✱

CHAPTER TWENTY FOUR

Bathroom

 erry and Claudia, a newly dating couple, claimed that they laughed through this entire section. She thought it was particularly funny that when Terry gets to the end of the toothpaste tube, he tears it open to be sure to use every last bit before throwing it away. When you are in a new relationship and not in the middle of a control battle, it is easy to see these things as insignificant and funny. But it will be interesting to check back in with them after they have lived together for a few years!

Some of the questions in this category are universally understood to be issues in relationships: Does he put the toilet seat down? Does she squeeze the toothpaste tube in the middle? Which way does the toilet paper go? We probably have Ann Landers to thank for bringing these issues into the public light! Remember, when "petty" things begin to really bug you, it may be a symptom of something bigger that is bothering you. Habits are hard to break, however, and a small offense here and there doesn't need to be the end of the world or the relationship. Often the issue isn't really what your partner is doing but rather that your need for approval or control is rearing its ugly head. Take a moment to self-observe, take a deep breath, and reconnect with your goals and values. Return to the equation, Event + Response = Outcome. Can you take a different approach with your partner that will bring about better results in your relationship?

What people consider acceptable ranges widely, and it does help to be with someone who sees things at least somewhat the same way as you do. At minimum, you want to find someone who is respectful of how you feel. I was at a banquet once, and after we all had finished the meal, one woman got out her dental floss right there at the table and began flossing her teeth—much to the other diners' dismay. On the same subject, I have received complaints that people find their partners' used dental floss all over the house. I also received a letter from a woman who complained that her partner thought it was hysterically funny to roll up all the windows in the car and then fart, laughing as she suffered through his gaseous expulsions. Similarly, others revealed that their partners would cover their heads with the blankets and pin them down while happily farting away. (What is it with this recurring theme?!)

When Steven and I discussed "the toilet seat" issue, he brought up a valid point. Who's to say that it is a man's job to be considerate of the woman's toilet seat preferences by putting the seat down, rather than the woman's job to be considerate of *his* preferences by putting the seat up? One compromise might be for both of you to close the lid completely each time you use it, requiring both partners to put it the way they prefer, rather than arguing about who is right and who is wrong.

While "his and her" bathrooms would eliminate some of these issues, that may not be realistic. In any case, practice self-observation and aim to be a good roommate. Be conscious of what you do and its effect on your partner. Also, observe your responses to your partner and choose actions and words that will facilitate the love between you, as well as your goals.

QUESTIONS TO ASK EACH PARTNER

❖ Do you squeeze the toothpaste in the middle?
   Do you roll up the tube as it gets used?

❖ Do you put the toothpaste cap on after using it?

❖ How often do you brush your teeth?

❖ Under what circumstances would you go to bed without brushing your teeth?

❖ Where do you leave your toothbrush? Do you put it in different places (on the counter, in the shower, in the kitchen, in a toothbrush holder…)?

❖ How do you feel about your partner using your toothbrush?

❖ Do you floss? Where (do you walk around the house flossing, etc.)?

❖ Where do you leave your used dental floss?

❖ How long do you spend in the bathroom each day?

❖ Is the bathroom a private place and time, or is it okay with you if your partner comes in and out while you are using it?

❖ How do you feel about sharing the bathroom (getting ready at the same time)?

❖ Do you shut and/or lock the door when using the bathroom?

❖ How often do you bathe or shower? Do you bathe in the morning, before bed, or both? What are your preferences and expectations about this?

❖ Do you like to shower together or alone?

❖ How often do you shampoo?

❖ Where do you put your wet towels?

❖ Is it okay with you to share towels, or do you want yours to be exclusively your own? How frequently do you get a clean towel?

❖ Do you ever take long baths or do other lengthy activities in the bathroom that may limit a partner's access to the bathroom (facials, manicures, shaving, etc.)?

❖ Which direction do you prefer the toilet paper roll to turn?

❖ How do you feel about conserving water by not flushing every time? (This may be a special concern in drought-prone areas.)

❖ Do you have any feelings or concerns around undergarments or laundry hanging in the bathroom to dry?

❖ Do you take the hair out of the shower drain or leave it? If you take it out, where do you put it?

❖ Do you leave hair in the sink (after trimming your hair or beard)?

❖ Do you trim your toenails/fingernails? Where do you leave the clippings?

❖ Do you leave reading material in the bathroom? If so, what kind?

❖ What is your morning and evening ritual? How do you get ready for the day or for bed?

❖ Are there things that you are very particular about when it comes to bathroom habits? Are you willing to negotiate on these issues?

QUESTIONS TO EXPLORE AS A COUPLE

❖ Who changes the toilet paper roll?

❖ Who cleans the bathroom? How often?

❖ Do you share toiletries (toothpaste, shampoo, etc.) or buy your own?

❖ Whose job is plumbing or clearing clogged drains?

OBSERVATIONS OF YOUR PARTNER

❖ Does your partner have bathroom habits with which you are comfortable/uncomfortable?

❖ What are your expectations around your partner's bathing and toothbrushing habits? Are you comfortable with their level of hygiene?

✳

CHAPTER TWENTY FIVE

Pets

'm a "cat person" and Steven is a "dog person." (A twist on the Mars/Venus theme!) Thus, when we got together, I wanted a cat and he wanted a dog. So we got both. Now he teases me about being a "dog person" because of how much I love Einstein (the dog). Steven, on the other hand, has grown to appreciate the cat as well. This is another case of how, when two people get together, their interests and lifestyles merge. It is a wise idea to take a look at how your partner feels about pets so that you know what you are merging with. It's a good thing, for my sake, that Steven isn't a "spider person"!

To some of us, our pets are as important as any other family members. To others, they are just creatures. Responsibility, kindness, and patience are just a few of the characteristics that may surface in interactions with animals. How your partner treats your beloved pets could certainly have an impact on the relationship. It may also show you something about how respectful they are toward others, or how they will treat children, or indicate their discipline style. I dated a man who completely lost control when my cat broke a lamp. I feared what his reaction would be if we ever had children and they made some kind of mistake.

When Wendee and Steve discussed these questions, Steve said that the most he thought it was appropriate to spend on an animal was about a hundred and fifty dollars. Wendee laughed and said, "I spent that much on my dog the first day I got her!" Another couple encountered a similar difficulty when their beloved dog required surgery on his back leg to the tune of twelve hundred dollars. They decided to go ahead with it, after which the dog promptly injured the other hind leg in exactly the same way. It was then that they discovered their limit.

Introducing your partner to your pets is always an interesting experience. Sometimes it is harder to get approval from a cat than it is from someone's children! When Cynthia brought her boyfriend home for the first time, she was embarrassed because her cat freaked out. Ordinarily, Sylvester spent the night on the pillow that was now taken over by this stranger. Making his displeasure known, the cat ran back and forth through the small apartment meowing until Peter finally got up and left in the middle of the night.

Pets tend to have a sixth sense about people, so if your dog can't stand your partner, pay attention—that may mean more to you than what your mother thinks of them! An unexpected problem can arise when partners begin to date and discover they are tremendously compatible, only to find out that she is totally allergic to his best friend, Rover. This poses a major question of priorities and tests problem-solving skills. Which will it be—the dog or the dog house?!

Questions to Ask Each Partner

❖ How do you feel about having pets?

❖ What kind and how many do you have?
   How important are your pets to you?

❖ Do you want to get (any or more) pets?
   What kinds of pets, and how many are acceptable to you?

❖ Are your pets substitutes for children?

❖ Are you allergic to animals?

❖ If your partner was allergic to your pet(s), would you be willing to get rid of them? (Which one—the partner or the pet?)

❖ Are you a "cat person," a "dog person," or neither?

❖ Are there any pets you would absolutely refuse to have (e.g., reptiles, rodents, strays, etc.)?

❖ Is it okay with you for animals to be in the house?

❖ Is it okay for pets to be on the furniture?

❖ How do you feel about feeding animals from your plate or at the table?

❖ What are your feelings about dogs or cats sleeping on the bed?

❖ How do you believe pets should be treated? How do you believe pets should be disciplined? Do you believe in hitting animals?

❖ Do you believe in getting animals vaccinated annually?

❖ Do you spay or neuter your pets, or do you let them have as many litters as they can produce? If so, what do you do with the babies?

❖ How do you feel about putting animals to sleep?
Under what circumstances would you consider it?

❖ If you were to go on a trip, what would you do with the pets (e.g., take them along, put them in a kennel, have a neighbor watch them, leave them alone, etc.)?

❖ What kind of environment do you provide for your pets? What are your feelings about tying an animal up or keeping it in a cage?

❖ How do you feel about feeding wild animals in your yard (birds, opossums, raccoons, etc.)?

QUESTIONS TO EXPLORE AS A COUPLE

❖ Who has the final word on whether to get a pet (or how many pets can be brought home)?

❖ Whose responsibility is it to discipline the animals? Is one of you naturally better at it?

❖ Do you have similar rules regarding what it is okay for a pet to do or not to do (e.g., enter the house or get on the bed, furniture, counters, etc.)?

❖ Whose responsibility is it to feed the animals?

❖ Whose responsibility is it to clean up after the pets? Clean cages? Repair damages? Walk the dog or clean the cat's box?

❖ Whose responsibility is it to bathe the pet? How do you feel about having the pet professionally groomed?

❖ Whose responsibility is it to take the pet to the veterinarian?

❖ How much are you willing to spend on a pet's medical treatment? Whose financial responsibility is it? How much do you think is appropriate to spend on other pet-related expenses?

❖ If you have children, how will you handle their desires for pets and the responsibilities involved?

❖ If you were to split up, who would get the pets?

Observations of Your Partner

❖ How does your partner treat (and talk to) their or your pets? How do they treat the pets when they are under stress?

❖ Does your partner take good care of their pets? Do they clean up after them and fix the damages that they may cause?

❖ How does your partner discipline pets?

❖ Do you think your partner's pet(s) are more important to your partner than you are?

Self-Observations

❖ Is your pet(s) more important to you than your partner is?

Observations of Your Pets

❖ Do your pets like your partner?

❖ Are they safe with your partner?

❖ Are you partner's pets friendly? Are they trained to be mean?

❖ Are they well taken care of?

✱

CHAPTER TWENTY SIX

Vehicles

ears ago, my parents gave me their old Buick to use while I was in college. As a surprise, they arranged to have it painted by a friend of our family's who had a business painting Mack trucks. Mom picked out a pretty sparkly blue color from a paint chip that she was sure I would like. In a tiny, one-inch square, the color was great and would have been perfect on a big truck. However, having a whole Buick painted a bright metal-fleck turquoise did absolutely nothing for my suave, sophisticated image—except with gas station attendants, who always loved it. I know, you're probably thinking, "She had an old blue school bus *and* a turquoise Buick?!" Remember, you can't always make assumptions about people because of what they drive—but it is fun to hear their stories.

At first glance, it wouldn't seem that vehicles are a necessary category in a relationship book. However, you can learn a lot about your partner by what they drive, how they drive, how they treat other drivers, and how they treat their vehicle. ("Vehicle" can be substituted with any means of transportation, e.g., bike, motorcycle, truck, etc.) For some, cars are a part of their identity.

How clean people keep their car is a topic that often comes up between partners. Liz tends to be the type who lets stuff (towels, sweatshirts, and trash) pile up in her car, while her boyfriend, Larry, keeps his vehicle immaculate and has to resist his desire to judge her. Her feeling is that she can keep her car any way she wants to and he has the same right with his.

Things changed when she got a convertible, because she had to keep it reasonably clean or everything would blow away (but don't look in the trunk)!

The issue of driving has also been an important one in many relationships. So much more is involved than mere transportation. It is an act of trust to be a passenger in a car. It is an act of responsibility to be a driver. One man I dated seemed really mellow until he got behind the wheel. He would swear and honk at people if they even remotely cut him off. One time he started racing after someone with me in the car, flipping them off because they changed lanes in front of him. That kind of loss of temper is a nonnegotiable item for me, and shortly thereafter we broke up.

In some relationships, particularly among people of older generations, the man was always the one to drive. Nowadays, the question of who drives can be decided in other ways than on the basis of gender . Mechanical care of the vehicles has also traditionally been more of a man's job. Agreeing on who will take responsibility for routine oil changes, tire checks, and tuneups can help to avoid a blame battle at the time of a breakdown.

Questions related to children and vehicles are in the "Children" chapter.

QUESTIONS TO ASK EACH PARTNER

❖ What is your primary mode of transportation (walking, bike, public transportation, car, etc.)?

❖ What is important to you in a vehicle?

❖ What are your needs for a vehicle (size, style, characteristics, etc.)? How many vehicles do you have?

❖ How important is your vehicle to you? Do you feel it makes a statement about you as a person?

❖ If money wasn't an issue, what kind of vehicle would you want?

❖ Do you own, or do you want to own, any recreational vehicles? If so, how do you use them? How often?

❖ How much care and time do you give your vehicle?

❖ How often do you wash/wax?

❖ Do you tend to let items or trash pile up in your vehicle?

❖ Is it okay for your partner, as a passenger, to put their feet on your dashboard?

❖ Do you allow eating, drinking, or smoking in your vehicle?

❖ Do you get car sick?

❖ Do you like to drive?

❖ Do you like going on long road trips?

❖ Do you mind asking for directions when you don't know where you are going?

❖ Do you get upset in traffic or with inconsiderate drivers? If so, how do you express your frustration?

❖ If someone cuts you off or is a disrespectful driver, how do you handle it, and how long do you let it bother you?

❖ Do you ever hitchhike?

❖ Do you pick up hitchhikers?

❖ Do you have a pet name for your vehicle? Are you particular about how your vehicle is referred to (e.g., "It's not a *car*, it's a *truck!*")?

❖ Will you let your partner drive your vehicle?

❖ Are you willing to let your partner drive you places?

❖ Are you comfortable driving with your partner (as passenger or as driver)?

❖ How do you respond when asked to drive more carefully?

❖ Are you a "back seat driver?"

❖ Do you do other things when you are driving (such as read, put on make-up, shave, talk on cell phones, etc.)?

❖ Are you mechanically inclined? Would you be willing to work on your partner's vehicle?

❖ Do you feel confident letting your partner work on your vehicle?

❖ Do you have car insurance? How do you feel about insurance?

❖ Do you ride motorcycles? If so, is it important to you that your partner also rides?

❖ Do you wear a helmet when bicycling or motorcycling?

❖ In a vehicle, do you wear seat belts? Do you insist that passengers in the vehicle wear seat belts or that small children are in car seats?

❖ Is it okay with you if your partner refuses to wear a seat belt or insists that you wear one?

❖ If your partner asks you to wear a seat belt (or helmet) when you normally do not, how would you respond?

❖ Do you ever drive under the influence of drugs and/or alcohol? Have you ever gotten a D.U.I.? If so, is it still on your record or affecting your ability to drive?

❖ Do you drink alcohol in the car when someone else is driving? When you are driving?

❖ Do you designate a driver when you go out? Is it always the same partner?

Questions to Explore as a Couple

❖ Whose vehicle do you, as a couple, generally use? Do you both need your own vehicles?

❖ Who drives when you go places? (Is it always the same person, or do you take turns?)

❖ Who is responsible for being sure that the vehicle's paperwork is up to date? Registration? Safety or smog checks?

❖ Whose responsibility is the mechanical maintenance of your car? Who checks the oil? How often?

❖ Whose responsibility is it to wash the car and clean its interior?

Observations of Your Partner

❖ Is your partner respectful of you and your comfort in the car?
Are they respectful of you both as a driver and a passenger?

❖ If you ask your partner to slow down or change the way they drive,
how do they respond?

❖ How does your partner treat other drivers?

❖ What does your partner's car and its condition say about them?

Self-Observations

❖ Do you feel safe in your partner's car?

❖ Is driving with your partner stressful or pleasant?

❖ Does it bother you if your partner leaves trash or belongings in
their car? In your car? If so, how do you respond?

❖ What does your car and its condition say about you?

CHAPTER TWENTY SEVEN

Plants
and Garden

hen Steven and I were looking to buy a home, we seriously considered one primarily because of its beautiful, lush vegetation. We then opted to buy a different home that met other needs. When that same house sold to another couple, the first thing they did was tear out all the vegetation and cut down the trees, much to our dismay.

People's attitudes about yards vary dramatically. Our expectations about our surroundings, and our aesthetic values, are often reflected in our yards or gardens. For some, plants are a critical aspect of their environment. For others, they are a nuisance and too much work. Chores around the yard and landscaping can have as great an impact as household duties on a relationship. Gardening can be considered meditative or agitating.

Our best friends have a manicured yard that looks like it belongs in a magazine. Although Steven and I are always impressed by its perfection, we also realize the amount of time and care such a yard requires. Our yard has a "natural look," where many of the plants choose where they want to grow and the mature trees provide an environment that makes our home feel peaceful. By contrast, other people on our street don't have a single plant in their yard, not even grass. Just as approaches to the yard vary from house to house, they can also vary from person to person. Each partner's attitude will certainly filter into the relationship.

Questions to Ask Each Partner

❖ How do you feel about plants in the house?

❖ How many plants do you like in the house?

❖ How much time do you spend in the yard?

❖ How do you use your yard? What activities take place there?

❖ How much time do you spend taking care of the yard?

❖ How do you feel about hiring a gardener?

❖ Do you have a preference for a garden theme (e.g., cactus, tropical, edibles, etc.)?

❖ How important is having a vegetable garden to you?

❖ How do you feel about the use of poisons and toxins in the house and in the garden?

❖ What are your beliefs about killing things in the garden (e.g., scorpions, centipedes, spiders, snakes, rodents, snails, slugs, etc.)?

❖ What does your garden mean to you? Do you have spiritual beliefs associated with your garden? Do you have medicinal or meditative approaches to gardening?

❖ Do you talk to your plants?

❖ How do you feel about statues or lawn ornaments in your yard? What kind do you like and how many?

❖ How do you deal with garden refuse? Do you let it pile up or take it to the dump?

❖ What is your level of tolerance for other items piling up in the yard, such as broken vehicles, etc.?

❖ How much land do you have—or how much would you want/require if you purchased or rented a home?

Questions to Explore as a Couple

❖ Does one partner have "ownership" of the garden, or is it shared?

❖ Whose responsibility is it to water the plants and take care of them?

❖ Who is responsible for yard work? Who is responsible for planting and landscaping?

❖ If you have a pool or Jacuzzi, who is responsible for its maintenance?

Observations of Your Partner

❖ Are your partner's garden preferences and beliefs compatible with your own?

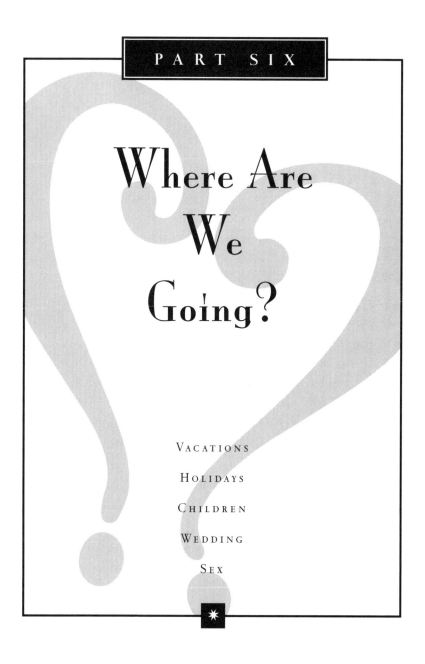

PART SIX

Where Are We Going?

VACATIONS

HOLIDAYS

CHILDREN

WEDDING

SEX

CHAPTER TWENTY EIGHT

Vacations

anya's goal for traveling is to visit sacred places and learn about the spiritual practices of the countries she visits. Her boyfriend, Todd, doesn't share the same interest but expects to go fishing no matter where they go. While Tanya likes to fish as well, she doesn't want to give up her interest in spirituality. Once they both accept the other's preferences, they will need to be willing to either do both or anticipate separate vacation times.

People often find that while they may get along in their day-to-day lives, they fight constantly on trips. Others find that they travel great together but don't get along at all in a normal daily work schedule. Spending twenty-four hours a day together, away from the comforts of home, creates new dynamics to explore. If your idea of the perfect vacation is to relax on a secluded beach with your partner, and your partner's idea of perfection is to go trekking in the Himalayas, this is valuable information to discover well in advance of the vacation! By talking it through beforehand, some compromises can be reached and problems prevented.

Traveling can bring up expectations and issues of respect, fear, safety, comfort, control, and finances, to name only a few. When Steven and I were at the airport on our honeymoon, getting ready to take off for Costa Rica, I was suddenly overwhelmed with the fear that I didn't know what to expect from him in a foreign country. I don't know why I thought he would be any different than normal, but the issues of not speaking the language well and not knowing the turf made me feel vulnerable.

Be especially aware if you meet (or met) your partner on a vacation. When people are on vacation, they are in a relaxed, low-stress situation. Living in Hawaii, we see tourists all the time who think that living here would be just like twenty-four hours a day of vacation. The reality is that people in Hawaii are working, while the tourists are playing. *Living* in a resort community is very different than *visiting* it. Tara moved to the mainland to be with Daryl, a med-student tourist whom she fell in love with while he was on a Maui vacation, sure that he was "the one." After a few short months, she returned, saying that Daryl wasn't the same in "real life." Things always look different when you're dealing with the stresses of daily life than they do when you're spending leisure time and money. So if you meet on vacation, take "real life" tasks and time schedules into consideration. That isn't to say that it can't work, as Steven and I met when I was on vacation! Just be aware of unrealistic expectations.

The questions in this book can help you on vacation as well as during the planning stages. One family took *Intellectual Foreplay* on a long drive and used appropriate questions to spur conversations with their adolescent kids. They found it a useful tool, not only for filling the time but for getting to know their children better. Another young man called and begged me to send him a book quickly for his upcoming road trip with a new girlfriend.

QUESTIONS TO ASK EACH PARTNER

❖ What kind of vacations do you like? What would be your ideal vacation?

❖ Do you like to travel? How important is travel to you? Is it a major feature of your life?

❖ If you're interested in traveling, where would you most like to go?

❖ Where have you traveled?

❖ Do you have a particular goal in mind when you travel (to see spiritual places, visit museums, participate in a sport or recreation, sightsee, relax, visit friends/family, see natural phenomena or historical places, etc.)?

❖ When you go on vacations, do you return to the same places year after year, or do you try to go somewhere new each time?

❖ Would you go somewhere that didn't interest you or somewhere you'd been before if your partner wanted to go?

❖ Do you try to see everything when you go somewhere, or do you stay in the same area and relax?

❖ Do you like to go camping/backpacking?

❖ Do you tend to take fancy, expensive trips or bargain, budgeted trips?

❖ Do you like passive vacations (such as cruises or sitting by a pool), active trips (such as biking across country), or risk-taking ones (such as trekking in the Himalayas)?

❖ What do you like to do to relax?

❖ What are the minimum amenities you require when traveling?

❖ Do you both tolerate conditions and inconveniences similarly?

❖ Can you really get away from work, or do you feel a need to call in every day or so?

❖ Do you tend to worry about the house or business while you're away?

❖ What is the minimum/maximum length of time you feel a vacation (traveling) should last?

❖ How much vacation time do you get off from work each year? How often do you go on vacation?

❖ Do you like to take weekend vacations?

❖ When traveling in a car, do you allow room for spontaneous side trips and exploration, or do you drive straight from point A to point B?

❖ How do you fill the time on long road trips?

❖ How do you feel about flying?

❖ Do you fly economy, business, or first class? Are you flexible about this?

❖ How do you feel about boat trips or cruises?

❖ Do you get sea sick? Motion sick?

❖ How do you feel about separate vacations?

❖ Do you travel on the spur of the moment/spontaneously, or do you require/prefer plenty of planning time?

❖ Do you tend to get to the airport (train station, etc.) with plenty of time to spare, or do you tend to arrive at the last minute?

❖ Do you save money for a trip and travel within your means, or do you use credit and pay it off when you get back?

❖ Do you plan your own trips or go with guided tour groups?

❖ When you go on vacation, do you get a housesitter? Who looks after your home?

❖ When you travel to foreign countries, do you try to learn some of the language before you go, or do you expect that they will be able to understand your language?

❖ Do you learn about the places you travel to before you go there?

❖ When you travel to foreign countries, do you tend to appreciate the different ways of the people, or do you find the differences strange or upsetting?

❖ Do you tend to travel light or pack everything you possibly can?

❖ Are you willing to carry what you pack, or do you expect your partner to do it?

QUESTIONS TO EXPLORE AS A COUPLE

❖ Who is in charge of planning vacations?

❖ Do you prefer traveling alone, with your partner, with your family, or in groups with lots of friends?

❖ Are you willing to go on vacations with your or your partner's family?

❖ When you go on vacations together, do you feel you should stay together the whole time, or do you go off to explore separately, reuniting later?

❖ How do you handle the finances on vacations?
Do both partners pay equally?

SELF-OBSERVATIONS

❖ Do you feel as though you and your partner will get along when spending twenty-four hours a day together on a trip, for a number of days in a row?

❖ Do you feel totally trusting and safe traveling with your partner? (Do you trust that they won't abandon you in unfamiliar surroundings or get into awkward situations with strangers? Do you trust their sensitivity and respect for other cultures?)

❖ Do you argue about directions or what activities you want to do on vacation?

❖ Do you argue over packing or how much to bring?

❋

CHAPTER TWENTY NINE

Holidays

Steven's family tradition was to open their Christmas presents on Christmas Eve. My family tradition was to open them Christmas morning. Rather than rationalizing our own ways of doing it, we found a compromise that we both like. On Christmas Eve, we open one present that is particularly special and then open the rest the next morning. In this way, we honor both traditions.

Holidays can be a time of joy or a source of pain and discomfort. Many people have very strong emotional attachments to holidays, both positive and negative. They seem to either passionately love them or hate them. Holidays often stir up old memories of the way things used to be, special occasions spent in other places and times and with other people. Because of these strong emotional feelings, expectations are also usually fairly strong.

The key to success in this area is to *communicate* (funny, just like all the other areas!). Taking a careful look at where you're compatible and where you're willing to compromise can give you an opportunity to create new traditions—together. Keep an open mind to new traditions and different ways of doing things, and look for creative solutions.

Corrine loves to decorate and spends hundreds of dollars on decorative items for every major holiday. Although her husband, Mike, doesn't mind the trinkets, they don't mean anything to him. He has decided that rather than resisting her style, he will appreciate Corrine's childlike enthusiasm.

One man, Lloyd, shared that after years of marriage he finally discovered a secret to making his wife, Joan, happy. In the past, Lloyd always waited until right before Joan's birthday to get her something, as giving and receiving gifts weren't a really high priority for him. What he discovered was that Joan loved to receive gifts—not because she wanted a present, but because the advance thoughtfulness represented to her that he cared about her. Now he buys the present a week in advance of her birthday, wraps it, and puts it out where she can see it all week long in anticipation but can't open it. This tiny shift in timeliness and consideration made a huge difference in their relationship. The more you know about yourself and each other's needs and desires, the greater your chances are of being happy.

Gift-giving and sharing special holidays are often very romantic. Consider these topics as they relate to the romance of your relationship as well.

QUESTIONS TO ASK EACH PARTNER

❖ Which holidays do you celebrate?

❖ Do you celebrate any special religious or cultural holidays?

❖ Do you have any religious beliefs that prohibit the celebration of certain holidays?

❖ Do you have a favorite holiday?

❖ How do you spend holidays (specifically the big ones: Christmas, Hanukkah, New Year's Eve, Halloween, Easter, etc.)?

❖ What are your traditions/expectations for holidays?

❖ How flexible are your customs and traditions for holidays?

❖ How elaborately do you decorate for holidays? How soon before and how long after the holiday do you think the decorations should be up?

❖ Do you entertain for the holidays? For friends, family, or work? If so, how elaborately?

❖ Do you get time off for the holidays, or do you have to keep working?

❖ When is your birthday?

❖ How do you feel about birthdays?

❖ How do you like to celebrate birthdays?

❖ How important are your birthdays to you?

❖ What do you expect from your partner on your birthday (not so much in terms of specific gifts, but rather in terms of levels of effort and attention)?

❖ What's your favorite birthday cake?

❖ How do you feel about surprise parties? Surprises in general?

❖ What are your favorite holiday memories?

❖ Do you tend to get sad around holidays?

❖ What are your expectations for Valentine's Day?

❖ What are your expectations for anniversaries?

❖ How important are anniversaries to you?

❖ Which anniversaries do you expect to honor (marriage, meeting, getting engaged, moving in together, first kiss, etc.)?

QUESTIONS TO EXPLORE AS A COUPLE

❖ Do you and your partner place a similar importance on holidays?

❖ Are your traditions compatible?

❖ Are you willing to co-create new traditions together? Have you already created some?

❖ How important is it that you spend holidays together?

❖ How important are gifts to you, both giving and receiving?

❖ How much do you spend on gifts? Is it an agreed-upon amount, or does it depend on individual preference? Should you each spend an equal amount?

❖ Who buys gifts for relatives?

❖ Do you give gifts to all your relatives, or do you all draw names?

❖ If you have divorced parents, stepchildren, multiple families, etc., how do you arrange your holiday time?

❖ Are you willing to spend holidays with your partner's family?

❖ Are you willing to let your partner go to their family's celebration without you?

❖ Are you willing to entertain your partner's family at your house? If so, how often?

❖ Who is responsible for sending thank-you notes and holiday greeting cards to family and friends? To the other person's family?

SELF-OBSERVATIONS

❖ Do you feel honored in the way that you deem appropriate for holidays and birthdays?

❖ Do you feel appreciated for the efforts you make to honor your partner?

❖ Have you and your partner already created new traditions together?

❖ Do you feel comfortable with your partner's level of respect for the spirit of the holiday you are celebrating?

❖ Do you associate gift-giving and/or any specific holidays with romance?

✱

CHAPTER THIRTY

Children

osh shared that he had a particularly challenging situation when he fell in love with Becky and her eight-year old son, Mickey. Not being the boy's true dad, Josh wasn't sure whether to be a father and disciplinarian or simply Mickey's friend. As time went on, they figured out their roles, and Josh and Mickey became very close. However, Becky and Josh began to have major problems and she stopped encouraging Josh and Mickey's relationship. Not only did Josh have a difficult time figuring out what his role in Mickey's life was as he entered the relationship with Becky, he also faced the challenge of figuring out what his role was with the boy as he and Becky split up.

In light of today's statistics about families and child-rearing practices, it would seem that some of the questions in this chapter should have been considered more by people long ago. If you are planning to have children, or if you have them already, remember that your choice of partners will not only affect you; you will be choosing a parent and role model for your children as well. This issue is very important, and the answers to these questions will help you avoid problems. Nowadays, chances are high that your potential partner will already have children from a previous relationship, which also creates unique dynamics of which to be aware.

As a counselor of adolescents and teenagers, I was tempted to put in a whole section of questions for the kids to ask you and your partner, but that would be another book. I spend my days listening to kids' concerns about their parents' choice of partners and the major effect it has on them—and their concerns extend to both their biological parents and their stepparents. The primary complaints I hear are about lack of attention—not feeling listened to or respected—and their parents' or stepparents' use of drugs and alcohol, and the bad temper or mood swings that go with this substance abuse.

> Imagine that your children—your current kids or those you may have in the future—are listening to each of your answers as you go through this section. Allow this image to help you self-observe and gain a different perspective on your beliefs and attitudes and choice in partners. Imagine that, after listening, they get to cast a vote, and pay attention to what you imagine they would say!

While sex obviously comes before children in a relationship, the chapter on children comes first in *Intellectual Foreplay* because the idea is to think about these questions *before* you choose to get married and/or have children. It is easy to romanticize the idea of having children when you think about cute cooing babies or adorable toddlers. The reality of raising kids is very different. Parenting brings strenuous times to a relationship. In addition, those darling children turn into teenagers, who have a notoriously difficult time getting along with their parents. It requires tremendous strength to handle these challenges with love and patience. If, after going through these questions, you don't think you and your partner are suited for parenting, not having children is a viable option.

All it takes to have kids is sex. They can be created in an instant, with no preplanning. It would make sense to issue parenting licenses that we could only acquire after taking courses, and perhaps getting a little therapy as well! However, in the absence of such a requirement, it is our responsibility to get educated, learn about ourselves, heal our past hurts, and choose partners who will contribute to a healthy family.

QUESTIONS TO ASK EACH PARTNER

❖ Do you have children from a previous relationship? If so, how many? How old? Do they live with you? If not, how often do you see them?

❖ Do you want children? How important is it to you to have children?

❖ What is your reason for having children?

❖ How many children do you want?

❖ When do you want children?

❖ Would you choose not to have children because of your age (too young or too old)?

❖ What age would you consider too young or too old for you to have children (physically, emotionally, or intellectually)?

❖ Are you willing to become a stepparent?
   What do you see as the responsibilities of that role?

❖ How do you feel about yourself as a role model for kids?
   Do you feel competent as a parent?

❖ What gifts (in terms of talents, wisdom, and beliefs) do you bring to parenting?

❖ Would you need a child of a certain gender to be happy?

❖ How, if at all, do you see raising a girl as different than raising a boy?

❖ Do twins run in your family?

❖ How would you feel about your partner donating sperm to a sperm bank or becoming a surrogate mother?

❖ Have you ever been guilty of abusing or molesting a child?

QUESTIONS TO EXPLORE AS A COUPLE

❖ How will your age difference, racial difference, or alternative sexual orientation, if any, affect your children as they grow up?

❖ How would you handle an unexpected or unwanted pregnancy?

❖ If you or your partner got pregnant and one of you wanted to keep the child but the other partner did not, what would you do?

❖ What are your feelings and beliefs about birth control, abortion, and/or adoption?

❖ How would you handle it if your partner was unable or unwilling to procreate? What if you were unable?

❖ What alternatives would you seek to have a child (artificial insemination, a surrogate mother, adoption, surgery, etc.)?

❖ Are you willing to or interested in going to childbirth classes?

❖ FOR THE FEMALE PARTNER: Do you want or are you willing to have your partner present and/or coaching at the birth of your child?

❖ FOR THE MALE PARTNER: Do you want to be or are you willing to be present and/or coaching at the birth of your child?

❖ Will you take maternity/paternity leave after the birth of a child? How much time are you willing to take off from work?

❖ In the case of differing last names, whose last name will the child take?

❖ Are there family names that one or the other partner are attached to naming their child? Do you both get a say in it?

❖ How do you think you would handle it if your child were born with a birth defect?

❖ What are your beliefs and attitudes about sharing childcare responsibilities? Are you willing to change diapers?

❖ Are you willing to get up in the middle of the night and early in the morning for your children?

❖ What are your beliefs on discipline? Who does the disciplining?

❖ How do you handle your anger when a child does something wrong? Do you believe in spanking? Yelling?

❖ How do you handle disagreements between you and your partner on the raising of the children?

❖ Do you think families should be run by one head of the household, by consensus, or democratically—with the children getting an equal vote?

❖ What kind of rules will you or do you have for your children/family/household?

❖ What do you consider quality time with a child?

❖ What do you see as a parent's role in a child's life?

❖ How much time do you think a parent should spend with their kids? Do your opinions on this differ depending on the age of the children?

❖ How much time are you willing to spend with your kids?

❖ How do you feel about both parents working?

❖ How will you balance out schedules and childcare if both parents are working?

❖ What religious beliefs will you pass on to your children?

❖ How do you show affection to children? Are you able to tell them that you love them? Are you able to hug them—even as they get older?

❖ What aspects of your childhood do you want to be sure your own children experience?

❖ What aspects of your childhood do you want to be sure your own children do *not* experience?

❖ Are you willing to go to parenting classes?

❖ How do you feel about children's education? Will you send them to public school or private school? Would you consider home schooling? Would you make decisions about where to live based on the reputation of the school system?

❖ How will you support or encourage your children in getting an education (e.g., helping with homework, reading aloud, etc.)?

❖ Will you both go to parent conferences and school functions?

❖ Whose responsibility is sex education?
How and when do you think it should be handled?

❖ How, if at all, will you or do you enhance your family's self-esteem? (See the "Self-Esteem" chapter for more detailed questions on this topic.)

❖ Do you see your family as functional and healthy?

❖ How do you feel about teenagers? Are you comfortable around them?

❖ How do you think you would prioritize your partner's needs and your children's needs?

❖ What are your beliefs and attitudes about doing drugs or drinking alcohol in front of the children?

❖ What are your views on letting teenagers drink, smoke, or do drugs? How do you imagine handling it if your teenager was using?

❖ How important do you think it is that children's opinions are heard? Teenagers'?

❖ What are your feelings on providing cars for your teenagers?

❖ How do you feel about allowing your children to have motorcycles, participate in off-road sports, etc? How do you feel about allowing them to participate in other dangerous sports?

❖ How protective do you think you will be (or are already) as a parent? How much freedom do you think kids should have?

❖ How do you feel about having your children participate in competitive sports or intensive competitions? Martial arts? Boxing? Modeling?

❖ What are your thoughts on giving kids an allowance? Is this conditional on doing chores, or should an allowance just be for spending money?

❖ Do you expect that children will do household chores?
If so, which ones?

IF CHILDREN FROM A PREVIOUS RELATIONSHIP ARE INVOLVED:

❖ How do you feel about bringing a new partner home to meet your kids? Are you hesitant for your partner and your kids to develop a relationship out of fear that your relationship won't last?

❖ How do you get along with your partner's child(ren)?
How do you get along with your own kids?

❖ Do you or your partner have any authority in disciplining the other's child(ren)?

❖ To what extent is a stepparent (or partner) expected to be responsible for entertaining or caring for the child(ren)?

❖ Are previous children a source of conflict in your relationship? Are you willing to confront, discuss, and compromise on these conflicts?

❖ If you both have children from previous marriages, or have children together and from previous relationships, how have you divided your assets in your will (e.g., half for his, half for hers, regardless of how many children, or in equal portions for each child)?

❖ If you have children from a previous relationship who don't live with you:

  • How often do you see your children?

  • How is your relationship with your children?

  • What is the likelihood that these kids will come live with you? How do you feel about that?

  • If the children suddenly needed to move in with you, how would it affect the relationship?

  • How is your relationship with the mother/father of your kids?

  • What are your obligations to your children (e.g., time, money, etc.)? Are you comfortable with those arrangements?

❖ If adult children from previous relationships are involved:

  • What is their role in your life now?

  • How does your partner get along with your children?

  • How does your relationship with your partner affect your relationship with your children?

  • How does your relationship with your children affect your relationship with your partner?

  • If the adult children were in need of a place to live, would you welcome them into your home? Would your partner welcome them? Would you welcome your partner's children?

- What is your financial involvement with your adult children?

❖ If you and your partner were to split up some day:

- How do you feel about paying child support? Would you pay it?

- Who do you think should have custody of the children; can you agree now?

- How do you feel about one partner putting down or bad-mouthing the other partner in front of the children?
  Can you imagine a circumstance in which you might do that?

OBSERVATIONS OF YOUR PARTNER

❖ How do you feel about your partner as a role model for your kids?

❖ What gifts or skills do you think your partner brings to parenting?

❖ How does your partner treat your children or children in general?

❖ How does your partner treat them when he/she is under stress or angry? Or when they are alone together?

❖ How is your partner's relationship with the mother/father of your kids? How is your relationship with your partner's former spouse? How does this affect your relationship with your partner?

❖ Are you comfortable with how your partner speaks about their former spouse in front of the kids? Are you comfortable with how your partner speaks about *your* former spouse in front of the kids?

SELF-OBSERVATIONS

❖ If you want children and your partner does not, are you willing to forego having them? If you don't want children and your partner does, are you willing to birth/raise children?

❖ Do you feel comfortable with your partner's family as role models (babysitters, caretakers) for your kids? If not, how do you intend to handle that? What about your own family?

❖ If you have children from a previous relationship, are you embarrassed or hesitant to introduce your partner to your children? How do your kids like your partner?

❖ Do you respect the way your partner disciplines their children?

❖ If your partner mistreated or abused your children, would you be willing or able to leave him/her?

❖ Is there jealousy between your partner and your children?

❖ Are you jealous of your children's relationship with your partner?

OBSERVATIONS OF THE CHILDREN

❖ Do the kids seem happy that you are together?

❖ Is the relationship between your kids and your partner (or between you and your partner's kids) stressful?

❖ Do the kids seem depressed? Do they show signs of anxiety or stress? Signs of abuse?

❖ Are the children able to express their feelings and opinions to you and/or your partner? Do they feel respected and honored?

❖ Are your partner's children well taken care of?

✳

CHAPTER THIRTY ONE

Wedding

I have been to a wedding in which the couple wore formal dress in an old Victorian house with a beautiful quartet. And to another on the beach in which the bride wore a white bikini and veil while the groom wore swim trunks and a bow tie. I attended yet another in which the bride and groom (and everybody else) were completely naked. I have been in a wedding in which I was the "best man" even though I am a woman, and I have performed weddings in Hawaii in a labyrinth, underwater, and on a boat. The variations and possibilities are endless.

We have heard many stories about couples who fell in love and happily planned to get married only to get into huge disagreements over the wedding plans. Getting married is something that starts to be planned when we are kids. Fairy-tale weddings are shared with us through books. Children look up to brides and grooms with wide eyes at the weddings they attend, as if they are looking at royalty or movie stars. Little girls sit around the playground at school and talk about what their weddings will be like. Then we grow up and meet a partner who has no intention of having a "royal wedding." In-laws also have their own ideas of what their son's or daughter's wedding will be like. Instead of planning a simple ceremony, you are dealing with issues of status, money, beliefs, desires, and philosophies. Suddenly, instead of needing a copy of *Bride Magazine,* you need *Psychology Today!*

Financial issues can also move into the forefront of a relationship during wedding planning. One couple, Julie and Ben, spent $50,000 (of her father's money) on their wedding only to divorce a couple of years—and a couple of kids—later. Some see the extreme expense of weddings as a waste of money that could be better spent on their livelihoods, while others figure they are planning the event of a lifetime and money should be no object.

Wedding styles also range tremendously. Consider what you want this memorable occasion to include, and discuss it with your partner to create an experience you'll both *want* to remember. Don't underestimate the importance of talking about the bachelor and bachelorette parties, and the impact they can have on your relationship as well. We have seen several weddings that were almost called off on account of them. It is wise, if you insist on having such an event, to do it well in advance of the wedding so that you have time to deal with any emotional reactions that may come up.

This chapter addresses the nuts and bolts of a wedding ceremony. The chapter on "Commitment and Trust" contains questions for exploring the ideas of marriage and monogamy and discovering whether marriage is desired by both partners. Questions on the celebration of anniversaries and gift-giving customs can be found in the "Holidays" chapter. Be sure to explore the "Vacations" chapter, too, when discussing your honeymoon!

 Describe your vision of the ideal wedding. Where would it be? How many would attend? Who would be the best man and the maid of honor? What would you wear?

Questions to Ask Each Partner

❖ How important is a marriage ceremony to you?

❖ What type and size of wedding do you want?
   What is your vision of an ideal wedding?

❖ How flexible are you on the type of wedding you will have?

❖ Would you consider an unusual wedding (underwater, skydiving, etc.)?

❖ Do you think a wedding should be a public display or a private exchange?

❖ How do you feel about eloping? Under what circumstances would you consider it?

❖ How do you feel about bachelor and bachelorette parties? What do you consider appropriate and inappropriate at these parties? What does this tradition mean to you? Are you willing to make changes based on your partner's concerns or discomfort?

QUESTIONS TO EXPLORE AS A COUPLE

❖ Who will be in charge of the wedding plans?

❖ What do you want the vows to say? How much do wedding vows mean to you? Do you want to write your own?

❖ How do you feel about the word "obey" in traditional vows?

❖ What are your feelings about the father giving the bride away? Will you include this tradition in your wedding?

❖ Who will be your best man, ushers, maid-of-honor, and bridesmaids? How many will you include?

❖ Where do you want to get married (which state, town, etc.; particularly if the families live in different locations)?

❖ Where do you want to get married: a church (what denomination?), outdoors, in a home, on a beach, etc.?

❖ Who will pay for the wedding? Does that person then have control over wedding plans?

❖ How much money do you consider appropriate to spend on your wedding?

❖ How do you draw the line between friends, acquaintances, and friends of the family in terms of who to invite?

❖ How do you feel about inviting former partners and spouses?

❖ If you are of different faiths, who will preside over the wedding? Will you limit the ceremony to one faith's rituals or create a combined ceremony?

❖ If your parents are divorced, how will you work out family photographs, who gives the bride away, and who pays for what?

❖ What are your preferences around the honeymoon?

❖ What do you think about the concept of renewing vows later in life?

❖ How do you feel about the woman taking, or not taking, the man's last name?

❖ How do you feel about hyphenated names or keeping individual last names?

❖ After marriage, do you think the woman should go by Ms. or Mrs.?

OBSERVATIONS OF YOUR PARTNER

❖ Does your partner consult you before making decisions that affect you?

❖ Are you experiencing interference from in-laws? If so, do you feel that your partner is supportive of you and your desires?

SELF-OBSERVATIONS

❖ Are your and your partner's expectations regarding weddings compatible?

❖ Are you and your partner able to stay strong in your relationship throughout this series of difficult decisions? Are you able to compromise on differences in preferences?

❖ Are thinking about and planning the wedding fun or stressful to you?

❋

CHAPTER THIRTY TWO

Sex

id you skip to this chapter before reading the rest of the book? If so, go ahead and satisfy your curiosity about yourself by reading the questions, but don't discuss them with a *new* partner until you've gone through the other chapters first. Exploring these questions first isn't *Intellectual Foreplay;* it is *physical* foreplay! It may very well lead to making the relationship too serious too fast. After you've looked at the questions, take a deep breath and go back to the beginning of the book. If you are already in a sexual relationship with your partner, at minimum, read Chapters One through Three and then go ahead and explore these questions—the sooner, the better.

If you and your partner have made it this far through the book and you are still together, chances are that you are extremely compatible on an intellectual, social, and spiritual level. Now is the time to discover your physical compatibility. This is the realm that separates best friends from lovers. Sexual compatibility, of course, will not be discovered in a serious discussion. A serious discussion can, however, improve your sexual compatibility. Personal identity, ego, judgment, expectations, and morality are all wrapped up in sexuality. Consequently, open, honest communication has to be handled carefully. Talking to each other, expressing your needs, respecting your partner's needs, keeping an open mind, and finding common ground are the ways to avoid underlying disappointments, resentments, and embarrassment.

Before you embark on the following questions, ask yourself about your intent. If you aren't looking for a lasting relationship, but rather just someone to have sex with, your approach to this section will be different, but be clear about that up front, as your partner may have a different goal. If you are looking for a long-term relationship, ask the questions with an intention to discover more about each other and your potential as partners. Refer back to the Foreplay exercises in Chapter Two that explore your current relationship goals.

Do you have a desire to know about your partner's past sexual experiences? *Be careful* about what you ask! Ask yourself if it would it bother you to find out that they'd had sex with someone of another race, the same sex, multiple sexual partners, extramarital affairs in previous relationships, premarital sex, abortions—or *all* of the above. What do you intend to do with the information once you've asked? By the same token, if your partner wants to know how many sexual partners you have had, *wonder why.* There is no purpose to this question, and it can only lead to judgment: either "too many" or "not enough." This question will elicit no answer to which someone will respond, "That's the exact answer I was looking for," unless maybe you answer that you haven't been with anyone else. Maybe. *Make sure your questions are purposeful and relevant.*

In this day and age of diseases, there is a certain amount of history that you may need to know, in addition to practicing safe sex, to protect yourself. However, your partner's *current* health status is more important and informative than how many previous partners they have had. The aim here is to learn about each other in reference to your *current* relationship, not to sit in judgment on each other. If the question does not have any relevance to the present, don't ask it. If you do venture into the past together, avoid throwing past experiences and decisions in the other person's face in a heated moment. Nothing can escalate a conflict more quickly.

Keep in mind that some of these questions are very direct. They are too direct for a first date or the beginning phases of a relationship. They are *not* too direct to discuss with someone who has already gone through the book with you or someone with whom you're already in a sexual relationship. As

Wendee put it, "These questions are no different than, 'Which direction do you want your toilet paper roll to turn?' It's a position issue—same question, different subject!"

Do not ask or answer questions that make you uncomfortable, but again, pay attention to what you or your partner are unable or unwilling to discuss. Also pay attention to what you both want to know. While discussing birth control and sexually transmitted diseases may seem to take the "romance" out of the experience, you should see what unwanted pregnancies and STDs do to the relationship! If you aren't mature enough to discuss these issues and take responsibility to avoid them, you aren't mature enough to have sex—no matter what your age.

Sex and lust create a certain level of insanity. People will jeopardize what is nearest and dearest to them for sex, lust, and love. All you have to do to really get a feeling for this is watch some of our talk shows or late-night shows on cable television that showcase the things that people will do—and will tell the rest of the world that they do! We are quick to judge other people's infidelities—at least until we are faced with that critical decision ourselves, usually at a moment when thinking is not our first priority. Apparently, in this day and age, there is an amazing variance in what people consider "normal" or "acceptable." The critical issues are what is normal and acceptable for *you*, what is normal and acceptable for *your partner*, and whether you are willing and able to meet each other's needs.

When I counsel people on the issue of sex, I emphasize that *the most important thing is respect*. Do you feel respected in how your partner treats you sexually? Do you respect your partner sexually? Even more importantly: Do you respect yourself sexually? If the answer is no to any or all of those questions, some serious reevaluation needs to take place.

Warning: These questions are meant to be asked of partners exploring a relationship. Do not open this chapter at work and start asking co-workers about their sexuality. This could constitute sexual harassment. Should a co-worker do this, take it as information about them, and be careful!

QUESTIONS TO ASK EACH PARTNER

❖ How comfortable or willing are you to talk about sex with your partner?

❖ Are you a virgin? If so, do you intend to remain one until marriage?

❖ What is your sexual orientation (i.e., heterosexual, homosexual, bisexual)?

❖ Are you comfortable with your sexual orientation? Do you ever question your sexual orientation?

❖ How do you feel about premarital sex?

❖ How do your religious beliefs influence your feelings about sex and sexuality?

❖ How comfortable are you with your sexuality? Do you feel guilty, promiscuous, conservative, fearful, satisfied, educated, naïve, etc.?

❖ If you haven't had sex with your partner yet, how will you know when the time is right? Are you waiting for some form of commitment, until you know each other well enough, until the spirit moves you, until the HIV tests return from the lab, until you get birth control, until you finish going through *Intellectual Foreplay,* etc.?

❖ How important do you think sex is in a relationship?

❖ How comfortable are you with nudity? In private? In public?

❖ In what ways do you think sexual involvement changes a relationship? (For instance, does sex change the level of commitment for you? Does the relationship's seriousness or importance change for you, or do you see sex as a casual exchange that doesn't mean anything in particular?)

❖ Do you equate sex with love (i.e., do you believe that if someone has sex with you, they love you, or that you must love them)?

❖ Is sex, for you, a means of expressing love or something done for physical satisfaction (in general and with your partner)?

❖ What are your spiritual beliefs about sex?

❖ What is your level of interest or understanding about sacred sex or sex as a spiritual experience, e.g., Tantra? What are your thoughts about sex being sacred? Is it something that you are willing to explore?

❖ Have you been tested for HIV/AIDS? When? What were the results? Have you recently been tested for other sexually transmitted diseases? If not, are you willing to be tested?

❖ Have you practiced "safe" sex?

❖ Are you willing to practice "safe" sex?

❖ Do you use birth control? What is your current method of birth control?

❖ Are you willing to use birth control?

❖ Do you share the responsibility of birth control, or is it one person's responsibility? Whose?

❖ Will your current method of birth control continue to meet your needs if sexual activity changes in frequency, becomes more spontaneous, etc? What are the disadvantages and advantages of that method? How do these affect your relationship/health?

❖ Are there any forms of birth control you're not willing to use?

❖ Are you willing to change your method of birth control, alternate methods, or alternate who takes responsibility for it?

❖ What are your beliefs about sterilization? Are you willing to get your tubes tied or have a vasectomy?

❖ On a scale of one to ten, rate your sex drive.

❖ How often do you want sex?

❖ When is your sex drive the highest (night, morning, afternoon)?

❖ Does your sex drive vary throughout the month?

❖ How do you engage your partner in a sexual experience?

❖ Do you think both people should initiate sex?

❖ Do you want your partner to be sexually aggressive or passive?

❖ How do you like to be kissed? How important is kissing to you?

❖ Do you have a pet name or nickname for sex or genitals? If so, what is it?

❖ How much or what kind of foreplay do you prefer? Is there anything you don't like in the foreplay stage of lovemaking (direct genital touching, ear kissing, etc.)?

❖ Is there anything that must be included in foreplay or lovemaking for you to be really aroused (e.g., kissing, talking, direct touching, ear kissing, eye gazing, etc.)?

❖ Do you prefer having the lights are on or off while you make love?

❖ Do you have a favorite place for making love? Where?

❖ Are you interested in having sex in different or unusual places (outside, in the vehicle, etc.)?

❖ What are your feelings and levels of desire or objection around these different sexual experiences:

  • Oral sex?

  • Masturbation?

  • Shared fantasies?

  • Anal sex?

  • Sex toys?

  • Porn movies/magazines/Web sites?

  • Bondage?

  • Voyeurism?

  • Threesomes or orgies?

  • Other??

❖ Do you have any fetishes?

❖ How much are you willing to experiment?

❖ Are there things that you're not willing to do?

❖ Are there certain positions that you prefer or dislike?

❖ Do you want or expect your partner to wear sexy underwear? How do you feel about wearing sexy lingerie?

❖ Do you tend to like spontaneous lovemaking? How do you feel about prearranged sexual encounters (e.g., Saturday morning is reserved for . . .)?

❖ Is it okay for the other person to say no to sex?

❖ If you wanted to have sex and your partner didn't, how would you handle it? Would you insist?

❖ When you don't feel like sex but just want to be held, how do you negotiate that?

❖ Is it okay with you to cuddle and be intimate without having it lead to sex?

❖ Are there times when you don't want to be touched? How do you express that to your partner?

❖ FOR WOMEN: Does your monthly cycle affect your desire to be touched?

❖ If your partner wants sex and you don't, do you feel obligated? Would you say something or just go ahead and make love? If so, do you make the best of it or feel resentful?

❖ How do you feel about your partner masturbating? When they are alone? During lovemaking? In front of you? Are you comfortable masturbating in front of your partner?

❖ Do you ask for what you want sexually? How do you let your partner know what you need?

❖ How do you respond when you don't get what you want?

❖ How do you like to be touched?

❖ Where are your erogenous zones?

❖ Are you able to have orgasms? Do you have any difficulty having orgasms? Do you have multiple orgasms?

❖ Do you expect an orgasm every time you have sex?

❖ Is it okay with you if your partner doesn't achieve an orgasm every time? (If it bothers you, do you think that this is because your ego is involved, or simply your desire to please your partner?)

❖ Can you give pleasure to your partner without expecting anything in return?

❖ How do you feel about receiving pleasure without reciprocating to your partner?

❖ Are there ways you'd like to improve in bed or things you'd like to learn more about?

❖ How much of your self-esteem is wrapped up in your sexual prowess?

❖ Do you talk to friends about the intimate details of your relationship?

❖ How would you feel about your partner talking to friends about the intimate details of your relationship?

❖ Are you willing to have sex during your/her period?

❖ How do you feel about sex during pregnancy?

❖ Do you have any bisexual tendencies or fantasies? Would you ever act them out?

❖ Do you read "adult entertainment" magazines? How do you feel about your partner reading them?

❖ Do you go to exotic dance bars or porn flicks? How often? Together, alone, or with friends?

❖ How do you feel about your partner going to strip shows or porn flicks?

❖ If your partner was seriously opposed to you going to these types of places, would you stop, go without telling, try to change their mind, or ignore their concerns?

❖ Do you frequent sex Web sites? Do you go into "adult" chat rooms?

❖ What are your thoughts and feelings about "phone sex" with
  your partner?

❖ Do you call 900 numbers and sexual-conversation phone lines?
  How would you feel about your partner doing that?

❖ Do you do anything or fantasize about anything "unusual" or
  not mentioned here that your partner ought to know about?

QUESTIONS TO EXPLORE AS A COUPLE

❖ If you haven't had sex yet, do you feel ready to have sex become
  a part of this relationship? How do you think sex will change your
  relationship?

❖ Who usually initiates sex?

❖ Are you currently satisfied sexually? Do you pay attention to each
  other's needs? Is satisfaction equal?

❖ Do either of you tend to use sex as a bargaining tool for getting your
  partner to do something for you or withhold sex to "punish" your
  partner? How do you feel about that? When is that legitimate negotiation, and when is it manipulation?

❖ Do you use sex as a prize in bets between you?

❖ Are you and your partner able to talk about these issues and make
  decisions together?

OBSERVATIONS OF YOUR PARTNER

❖ Does your partner touch you in a loving and nurturing way?

❖ Does your partner ask for what they want?
  Do they ask you what you want?

❖ Does your partner pay attention to whether you are satisfied?

SELF-OBSERVATIONS

❖ Are you comfortable with your partner's sexual interests
  and behaviors?

❖ Do you feel safe with and respected by your partner?

❖ Do you respect yourself when you have sex with your partner?

❖ Does one of you take more of a lead in your sex life?
  Are you comfortable with that?

❖ Does your perception of yourself (your appearance, weight, etc.)
  affect your sexuality? If so, what are you willing to do about it?

❖ Are you comfortable with the way your partner requests sex
  or speaks about it?

❖ How do you feel about your partner talking "dirty"?
  Do you like it, or does it offend you?

❖ Are you satisfied with the level of intimacy you share during
  lovemaking?

❖ Is your sexual relationship with your partner a toxic one or
  a nourishing one for you?

PART SEVEN

Can We Evolve Together?

QUESTIONS TO ASK YOURSELF

BRINGING OUT THE ELATION
IN rELATIONships

CHAPTER THIRTY THREE

Questions to Ask Yourself

ne woman, Renee, shared that she went through *Intellectual Foreplay* with her partner and that they discovered major areas of compatibility. Nothing she encountered raised an obvious red flag about continuing their relationship. When she got to this section, however, one simple question—"How do you feel about yourself when you are with your partner?"—revealed to her a discomfort that she felt when she was with him that she didn't recognize until she was asked to self-observe. She shared that she always felt on edge, like he was judging her, and consequently she never felt that she could be herself. Not sure whether this was a self-esteem issue for *her* or an attitude problem for *him,* she decided to hold off on getting serious until she could do a little more self-observation in other situations.

A gentleman by the name of Don discovered some areas of incompatibility with his girlfriend, Lila, as they went through the book. When he went through this section, though, his overall feeling was that the benefits of being with her far outweighed their differences. Because they had both been practicing self-observation and *choosing* healthy responses to each other when situations came up, he felt that they would be able to overcome the obstacles.

You are encouraged to read through this chapter before you have gone through all the other question chapters and to read it again afterward. Virtually every question in the book can be asked of yourself as well as your partner. The questions below, however, are specifically designed to help you take a look within and to assist you with self-analysis, self-clarification, and decision-making. Some of these questions could easily go into the observation sections of other chapters, but they are highlighted here to add emphasis as you review all that you have learned about your partner. You'll want to ask yourself some of these questions before you get seriously involved, while others should be asked after you are already together and deciding whether to take your relationship to the next level.

❖ How do you feel about yourself when you're with your partner?

❖ How do you feel about yourself when you're *not* with your partner?

❖ Ask yourself:

- What's it like to be in a relationship with me?
- What's it like to wake up with me?
- What's it like to make love with me?
- What's it like to raise children with me?

❖ Are you a toxic or nourishing person—to others and to yourself?

❖ Do you feel your partner is a toxic or nourishing person?

❖ Why do you stay in this relationship? What are its benefits?

❖ Do you "want" a partner or "need" a partner? Explain.

❖ What is the cost of being in this relationship? Consider the following:

- Will you have to move?
- How much freedom do you have?
- How does the relationship affect your friendships?
- How does the relationship affect your family relationships?
- How does the relationship affect your spirituality?
- How does the relationship affect you financially?

❖ In general, is your partner a positive or negative influence on you?

❖ If attitude were contagious, would you want to catch your partner's?

❖ Do you consider your partner your friend?

❖ Do you trust your partner?

❖ Are you trustworthy?

❖ Does your partner hurt you (physically or emotionally)?
Do you feel safe with your partner, both physically and emotionally?
Are you scared of your partner? Do you ever feel afraid when you're
with your partner?

❖ Do you feel loved by your partner? Do they communicate love to you?

❖ Is your partner considerate of your feelings?

❖ Is your partner a compassionate person?

❖ Are you embarrassed to have your friends or family meet
your partner?

❖ Are you proud of your partner and how they live their life?

❖ What things do you like about your partner?

❖ Do you respect your partner's opinions and the way they
express themselves?

❖ Do you respect your partner's intelligence, wisdom, and
problem-solving abilities?

❖ Would you feel safe leaving major life decisions in your partner's hands

❖ Do you and your partner solve problems in a way that is satisfactory to both of you?

❖ How do you and your partner handle conflict?

❖ Can you and your partner apologize and admit when you are wrong?

❖ Do you have goals for your future? Can you reach them within this relationship?

❖ Are there areas of your life that are not in alignment with your beliefs and goals?

❖ Do you believe your relationship is assisting you toward your goals, or is it a distraction or obstacle to your goals?

❖ Does your partner have goals that they can meet within the relationship?

❖ Do you support each other's goals?

❖ In general, are you comfortable or satisfied with the way your partner does things?

❖ Does your partner treat you as though they are comfortable or satisfied with the way you do things?

❖ Of all the things you know about your partner, what do you consider to be their most important (both positive and negative) traits?

❖ What can you let go of as unimportant concerns?

❖ What are the implicit (i.e., unspoken) agreements between you? Can you make them explicit?

❖ Which agreements are so important that you would break up if they were violated?

❖ How willing is your partner to talk with you about feelings?

❖ How willing are you to talk with your partner about feelings?

❖ Did you allow your partner to answer all the questions freely, or did you make assumptions, "knowing" what they would say without asking them?

❖ Was there anything they wouldn't discuss with you?

❖ Did you really listen to (hear) your partner's answers?
Did you pay attention?

❖ Was there anything you weren't comfortable asking but wish you knew?

❖ Were you really honest in answering, or did you say what you thought your partner wanted to hear?

❖ What was your motivation for asking or answering the questions? Was it to be entertained, increase knowledge, find reasons not to be together (because you have doubts), find proof that you should be together (reassurance), spur personal growth, etc.? Pay attention to your reasons.

❖ Do your partner's answers match their actions?

❖ Are you getting what you want out of this relationship, or are you settling for less? Is there anything you're yearning for in the relationship that you're not getting or anything in life that you're yearning for that you can't get if you are in this relationship?

❖ Are you comfortable being alone or scared of being alone?

❖ How much does not wanting to be alone contribute to your decision to be in this relationship?

❖ Do you trust your partner's use of and attitude about money?

❖ Do you often feel abandoned or avoided by your partner due to excessive withdrawal into computers, television, books, alcohol, work, or other activities? If so, can you tell them?

❖ How similar or dissimilar were your upbringings? Do you see this affecting the relationship?

❖ Do you and your partner have an "Attitude of Gratitude" toward each other and life in general? Do you each show appreciation for the other's efforts?

❖ Do you feel appreciated by your partner?

❖ After finding out all the things you now know about yourself and your partner, is there anything that you want to change?

❖ Would you be willing to stick around if those changes were not made? Could you be happy anyway?

❖ In your heart, do you feel that you are making the right choice by being in a relationship with your partner?

❖ In your heart, do you feel that *you* are the right choice for your partner?

CHAPTER THIRTY FOUR

Bringing Out the ELATION in rELATIONships

*"Keep your eyes wide open before marriage,
half-shut afterwards."*

— BENJAMIN FRANKLIN

he word "elation" is embedded right in the middle of "relation-ship." It hides there, unnoticed, just as the feeling itself gets hidden in relationships when we become bogged down with day-to-day challenges, conflicts, and insecurities. Elation is defined as "raised or lifted up, having the spirit lifted up as with success." It is the joy that happens when your spirit is touched. Engaging in *Intellectual Foreplay* can help you continue to touch each other's spirits over time.

Intellectual Foreplay doesn't need to be restricted to making a decision about a partner. You can engage in it throughout your relationship to help resolve issues that come up and to foster deeper levels of communication and intimacy, bringing you back to love, back to joy, and back to living in alignment with your goals and values.

When we get wrapped up in the busy-ness of our lives, it is easy to forget to mute the television when our partners are talking, or to spend a few minutes debriefing the day, or to take some time to discuss philosophical ideas that stir our souls, or to look past the little things that bug us toward the big things that matter to us. Keeping a relationship joyful requires giving it time and attention. By returning to the key concepts shared in *Intellectual Foreplay*— self-observation, getting refocused on our goals and values, choosing responses in alignment with what we want to create, and communicating (both sharing and listening, asking and answering)—we can create a relationship that is mutually satisfying.

It is also valuable to return to the questions from time to time to get to know each other more deeply or to re-negotiate certain aspects of your relationship. With the addition of life experience and new information, some of your answers will change over time. We've all heard people say, "I just don't know him any-more..." when referring to an estranged partner. People can change. But by periodically and playfully returning to *Intellectual Foreplay*, you can stimulate the relationship by continuously getting to know each other better. Make change conscious and something to celebrate rather than something that just happens when no one is looking.

It is helpful to recognize that feelings in relationships are cyclical. There will be times when you feel close to your partner and times when you feel a million miles apart. There will be times when you cherish them and times when you can barely tolerate them. Knowing that this cycle is a natural process can help you to be prepared for it. When you get into an unconscious pattern of resisting your partner, you can unconsciously send the relationship into a tailspin. By observing yourself and settling your intentions, you can choose responses that re-ignite the loving feelings between you.

When you are in a long-term relationship, it is necessary to take some active steps to "fall in love" again and again, to restore the joy and elation in being together. Whether we want to love a lifelong partner, our children, our parents, or ourselves, the recipe for falling in love is the same. Love comes from talking with each other, sharing experiences together, sharing feelings, sharing laugh-ter, touching each other in nurturing ways, being honest and considerate with each other, respecting each other, helping each other to do and to be our best, doing nice things for each other, and appreciating each other. Love comes from FOURplay: sharing ourselves mentally, emotionally, physically, and spiritually.

One of the things that comes with being in a relationship is conflict. It is part of the package. If you went through the process of *Intellectual Foreplay* with a partner, you have shared more with each other than most couples ever do. You have consciously chosen to be together rather than doing so simply out of convenience. For Steven and me, going through *Intellectual Foreplay* established a true and deep friendship upon which to build our relationship. The same was true for Wendee and Steve. There is a strength that comes from this level of awareness, and you can draw upon that strength when navigating disagreements.

Conflicts are one of the primary things that get in the way of our loving feelings toward our partners. As children, when someone is angry with us, we think they don't love us anymore, not recognizing that love and anger can and *do* coexist within the same person at the same time and that those emotions can be directed at the same object. As we grow up, we continue to battle feeling simultaneous love and anger for those with whom we are in relationships. When we encounter anger, it is important to look beneath it and express the full range of emotions that accompany it rather than just the anger. Just the act of observing ourselves and acknowledging the range of emotions we feel begins the process of releasing them. Thus we can move through the painful feelings and get back to love rather than getting stuck. When we are back in love, we are in a much more flexible place and are prepared to explore the myriad creative solutions available for resolving conflicts and making agreements.

Anger is like a flag on top of a mountain of other emotions. It doesn't exist all by itself. Several other emotions also affect us. Directly under anger is *hurt*. When we are mad at someone, we also feel hurt by them or the situation in some way. It hurt our feelings that they didn't consider us; it made us sad that they didn't trust us; etc. Underneath hurt is *fear*. We are afraid of losing the relationship, afraid of what others will think of us, afraid that we will continue to be hurt, afraid that we will never be able to trust again, afraid that we are being made to look foolish, and on and on. We are afraid of losing control or losing approval. Our need for control is embedded in anger, and our need for approval in hurt. Both are hiding in our fears. When we look at these through self-observation and transcend them, we can return to giving and receiving love.

Underneath fear is *responsibility*—or a sense of remorse for our part in the situation. It is rare to encounter a conflict or circumstance that we do not have some responsibility for, even if it is simply being in the wrong place at the wrong time. When expressing the whole truth of our feelings, it is very empowering to admit to ourselves and to let our partners know what we are sorry for and what we could have done differently. Again, it is in our "response-ability" that the power for healing and change lies.

When we let go of blame to the extent that we can recognize our responsibility in a situation, we are then able to have a sense of *understanding*. In other words, when we drop our guards of defense and resistance for a moment, we can feel some compassion for what the other person is experiencing. From a place of understanding, we can see parts of why our partner, friend, or family member did what they did, or we can see what the *misunderstanding* was that contributed to the situation. When we take a moment to try to see it from their side and to take in all the information, we are better able to understand the situation.

Once we reveal our responsibility for and understanding of the situation, we can share what we want. We want to be treated fairly, we want a loving relationship—or we may want out. Regardless, by *expressing* our desires, half the battle of achieving them is accomplished. By the same token, our partner will be better able to hear about our desires when they feel understood.

Underneath what we want is *appreciation, forgiveness, and love.* This level is easier to see when we're dealing with partners or family members rather than total strangers, but even when we don't know the person we are angry at, on the soul level we care about them as human beings. With our loved ones, however, it is much easier to recognize and express what we love and appreciate about them, which can then lead us toward forgiveness.

What we often do when we are unaware of all these underlying emotions is express only our anger or hurt to our partner. They then express their anger, hurt, and defensiveness back to us—which is a very difficult place to reach agreement from. The conflict then goes back and forth on the top of the emotional mountain without ever getting any closer to resolution. When you have a conflict with a loved one, allow yourselves to think through, feel, and express all your feelings rather than just the anger. When we just express the anger and hurt, the trail often leads toward hatred rather than back to love. When we express our full range of emotions—anger, hurt, fear, responsibility, understanding, want, and love—we can then begin the process of negotiation and agreement. **The bottom line is love.**

When you encounter a conflict, recall these sentence stems, and when you are ready, share your feelings with your partner. Ask them to listen to all your feelings before responding, and encourage them to use the same format as you listen to them.*

I felt angry when...

I was hurt that...

I am afraid that...

I am sorry for...

I understand that...

What I want is...

What I appreciate about you is...

After you have both expressed the full range of your feelings—and *listened* to each other—see if you can come to an agreement.

What I'd like to agree to is...

---

* Adapted from Jack Canfield's "Self-esteem in the Classroom" Curriculum Guide.

This is a great tool for releasing built-up emotion over past relationships, too. Even if you never share your feelings with a former partner, the process of writing them down will help you to release them and return to love.

Intellectual Foreplay is about using your head and your heart. *When you return to your heart—to love—you can use your head to create a relationship built on compassion and respect.*

Having respect for yourself and your partner and being respected by your partner are crucial for a nourishing relationship. Respect is accessible when you take the time to self-observe, become aware, and choose actions and words that are in alignment with the goal of love. The following chart can be used as a recipe for respect. The more we make these statements true, the more joyful we will be in our relationships with others.

RESPONSIBLE: I take responsibility for all my thoughts and actions.

ENTHUSIASTIC: I participate fully, sharing my spirit and heart.

SUCCESSFUL: I give everything I do my best effort.

PURPOSEFUL: I have a conscious purpose for all my words and actions.

ENCOURAGING: I support myself and others in doing our best.

COMMUNICATIVE: I create intimacy by sharing my feelings and thoughts.

TEAMMATES: I am part of a team, working together for the good of all.

FRIENDLY: I am kind and considerate of myself and others.

UPSTANDING: I am honest and honorable, and I have integrity.

LOVING: I am here to learn, laugh, and love.

Love Is the Bottom Line

The key to bringing out the elation in relationships is to remember that the bottom line is love—always. In all our relationships with others, the bottom line is love. In our relationships with ourselves, the bottom line is love. In our relationships with nature, the planet, the environment, its creatures, the bottom line is love. In our relationship with our jobs, the bottom line is love. In our relationship with our children, the bottom line is love. Love is a state of awareness, a remembrance. When we remember love and respect, we are appreciative. Appreciation contributes to thriving, elated relationships. This remembrance may need to be a conscious effort in the beginning, but it will become habitual and everlasting.

Establishing this awareness of love, respect, and appreciation is a process, as is change. Become aware of what you say, what you think, and what you do—your words, thoughts, and deeds. This requires a conscious effort to pay attention. Catch yourself. Observe yourself. Listen to yourself. When your words, thoughts, and actions are not aligned in love, re-think them, re-say them, re-do them. Set your intention on love. When you do what you do with love, you will see that love reflected all around you. Remember E + R = O. It is always your response that makes the difference in the quality of what you are experiencing. The choice to "resist what is" or to nag, tease, and use sarcasm and put-downs will *always* result in the death of love and happiness.

One way to restore love or to bring out the elation in a relationship is to look for the good in your partner instead of the bad. This is an important aspect of raising your own self-esteem as well. *Treat yourself and your partners in life like a gold mine.* When a miner goes into a mine to find gold, he has to remove tons and tons of dirt and rock to even find a single nugget, but he never, ever goes into the mine looking for the dirt. When we focus on looking for the dirt in our partner or ourselves, we will undoubtedly find some. The more we look for it, the more there will be to judge. The more we look for the good, the more we will see to appreciate. The more you acknowledge what you appreciate, the stronger those good qualities will become. This requires you to make a subtle, yet conscious, shift in your awareness and make an effort to re-set your intention on love and appreciation—on acceptance rather than resistance.

The process of awareness and change may not be instantaneous. You may find that, as you go through your day, you are unconscious of what you are saying, thinking, and doing. Once awareness is sparked, you will move through your day and catch yourself right *after* you have said, thought, or done an unloving thing. You will have done it, but you will be *aware* that you did it.

Set your intention again on love. Next, you will move through your day and become aware of what you are doing, saying, or thinking *right in the middle* of the act. Awareness is coming sooner, yet not soon enough to change the action— momentum will have already taken over. Again, in contemplation, re-set your intention on love. Then you will find that *just as you enter* into the unloving words, thoughts, or deeds, you become aware. Again, awareness is coming sooner, but not soon enough to fully counteract the momentum, although you may make some slight recovery of the situation in an effort to move toward love. In afterthought, set your intention again on love. Next, you will find that just *before* you enter into the unloving state, you catch yourself, make a conscious choice to act from a state of love instead, and change your thoughts, words, and actions. You will rejoice in your victory of conscious change and again set your intention on love. Next, as you move through your day, you will unconsciously choose an entirely different path, one lined with love, so that no conscious choice to move away from any other state is necessary. The state of love has become your home territory. You own it, you live there—the change is complete. Although little side ventures may present themselves, a simple restating of intention will be all that is necessary to stay on this new highway, your path of love.

The power to have a joyful relationship is within your grasp. Remember that the key to *making* the right choice is first *being* the right choice. Being the right choice includes having healthy self-esteem and treating yourself and your partner with respect. Making the right choice requires being conscious, asking questions, and paying attention to what you think and how you feel.

Our prayers are with you. May the elation and joy that you contain within be revealed to you and those around you. May you experience the powerful, loving strength that you hold for making the right choice and being the right choice in partners. May the process of *Intellectual Foreplay* be the juice of life, bringing you all the intimacy, elation, and love you deserve.

✳

Send us your stories!

❖ How did you use *Intellectual Foreplay* and what were the results?

❖ What were your funniest dates? Most embarrassing dates? Most romantic dates?

❖ What "Little Red Flags" have you encountered on dates? (You know, those little warning signs that let you know that the relationship should go no further!)

❖ Did you generate a list of questions that we didn't include? What are they?

❖ What are your success stories? How has *Intellectual Foreplay* helped you make the right choices?

You can send your stories by email to:
hhi@hunterhouse.com

or by U.S. mail (typewritten, please) to:
Eve Hogan c/o Hunter House Publishers
P.O. Box 2914, Alameda CA 94501-0914

Wings to Wisdom
TOOLS FOR SELF-MASTERY

Other Books and Tools for Self-Mastery
by Eve Eschner Hogan

RINGS OF TRUTH
by Jim Britt with Eve Eschner Hogan

A novel in the genre of visionary fiction in which an ethereal woman, Alea, guides both the main character and the readers to discover the keys to letting go of control and approval issues, and gaining a deep sense of resourcefulness in their lives.

THE WAY OF THE WINDING PATH:
A map to the spiritual journey of life...

reveals lessons from walking the labyrinth, a beautiful, 12th century pattern tiled into the floor of the Chartres Cathedral in France. This book leads the reader on the mystical journey of life guided by this metaphorical pilgrimage.

THE PLEASURE PRESCRIPTION: To Love, to Work, to Play—Life in the Balance by Paul Pearsall, Ph.D.

New York Times Bestseller!

This bestselling book is a prescription for stressed out lives. Dr. Pearsall maintains that contentment, wellness, and long life can be found by devoting time to family, helping others, and slowing down to savor life's pleasures. Pearsall's unique approach draws from Polynesian wisdom and his own 25 years of psychological and medical research. For readers who want to discover a way of life that promotes healthy values and living, THE PLEASURE PRESCRIPTION provides the answers.

288 pages ... Paperback $13.95 ... Hard cover $23.95

WRITE YOUR OWN PLEASURE PRESCRIPTION: 60 Ways to Create Balance & Joy in Your Life
by Paul Pearsall, Ph.D.

For the many readers who have written asking for ways to translate the harmony of Oceanic life to their own lives, Dr. Pearsall offers this companion volume. It is full of ideas for bringing the spirit of *aloha*—the ability to fully connect with oneself and with others—to everyday life. Pearsall encourages readers to feel the pleasure that comes from making joy a part of each day.

224 pages ... Paperback ... $12.95

PARTNERS IN PLEASURE: Sharing Success, Creating Joy, Fulfilling Dreams—Together by Paul Pearsall, Ph.D.

In this new book, Dr. Pearsall continues his exploration of *aloha* and the health and emotional benefits of a healthy balance of play, love, and work to present a plan for a committed, long-term relationship. This includes
  ❖ a mutual mission statement
  ❖ a partner's plan for the relationship
  ❖ 8 lessons in *mahele* (sharing)
Many relationship books focus on personal power or fulfillment. PARTNERS IN PLEASURE returns us to the task of becoming the right partners together, a lifelong adventure that strengthens and sustains each partner even as it brings harmony and peace to all those around them.

288 pages ... Paperback ... $14.95 ... Publication: APRIL 2001

To order books see last page or call (800) 266-5592

SEXUAL PLEASURE: Reaching New Heights of Sexual Arousal and Intimacy by Barbara Keesling, Ph.D.

This book starts with the first principle of intimacy: to experience deep sexual pleasure, you must explore your ability to enjoy relaxed, anxiety-free caressing. Exercises are done both with and without a partner to increase your sensual awareness and enable you to experience sexual ecstasy. SEXUAL PLEASURE is unique in encouraging you to focus on your own sexual desire, rather than looking for ways to please your partner.

224 pages ...14 b&w photos ... Paperback $13.95 ... Hard cover $21.95

MAKING LOVE BETTER THAN EVER: Reaching New Heights of Passion and Pleasure After 40
by Barbara Keesling, Ph.D.

Contrary to popular myth, great sex is not reserved for those under 40. With maturity comes the potential for a multi-faceted, soulful loving that draws from all we are to deepen our ties of intimacy and nurturing. In this book, sex expert Barbara Keesling provides a series of exercises that demonstrate the power of touch to heighten sexual response and expand sexual potential; reduce anxiety and increase health and well-being; build self-esteem and improve body image;open the lines of communication; and promote playfulness, spontaneity, and a natural sense of joy.

208 pages ...14 b&w photos ... Paperback $13.95 ... Hard cover $24.95

SENSUAL SEX: Awakening Your Senses and Deepening the Passion in Your Relationship
by Beverly Engel, MFCC

All of life is a sensual experience. While we live in a highly sexual culture, it is not very attuned to sensual pleasures. SENSUAL SEX shows readers that by becoming more attuned to their five senses, they can develop an increasingly erotic relationship with their body and their partner's body. Through a series of innovative touching and sensuality exercises, SENSUAL SEX helps couples reconnect with their bodies, heighten the excitement of new love, and put the spark back into long-term relationships.

256 pages ... Paperback $14.95

To order books see last page or call (800) 266-5592